D0820523

REAGANOMICS

A Midterm Report

REAGANOMICS

A Midterm Report

Edited by

Wm. CRAIG STUBBLEBINE
and THOMAS D. WILLETT

ICS PRESS

Institute for Contemporary Studies
San Francisco, California

Inquiries, book orders, and catalog requests should be addressed to ICS Press, Suite 811, 260 California Street, San Francisco, California 94111—415—398—3010.

Library of Congress Cataloging in Publication Data
Main entry under title:

Reaganomics: a midterm report.

     Includes index.
      1. Supply-side economics—Addresses, essays, lectures.
2. United States—Economic policy—1981—   —Addresses, essays, lectures. I. Stubblebine, William Craig.
II. Willett, Thomas D.
HB241.R37 1983   338.973   82—25844
ISBN 0—917616—54—5

CONTENTS

PREFACE

Toward the end of the 1970s, concerns about the U.S. economy were expressed with increasing frequency by policymakers and scholars of all political persuasions. Persistent high inflation and unemployment, combined with sluggish or nonexistent productivity growth, produced the worst decade of economic performance since the Great Depression.

In the fall of 1980, Ronald Reagan was elected president largely on the basis of his campaign promise to do something about the economy—especially to restore the growth that Americans had taken for granted for most of their history. "Supply-side economics" came to designate those policies designed to restore economic incentives to work, save, and invest—and thus to create an environment conducive to renewed growth. It is not too much to say that the Reagan administration has sought to bring about the most fundamental change in attitudes toward the function of government since the New Deal.

Although "supply-side economics" meant different things to different people, Ronald Reagan received a mandate to implement his particular version. This involved major tax cuts, federal budget control, deregulation, and important changes in monetary policy and federalism.

While it is clearly too early to give a final judgment on the Reagan program, it is evident that although it has attained one of its major and most difficult objectives—that of curbing inflation—it has not produced the rapid results for the overall economy hoped for by the administration. Now, at the administration's midpoint, questions arise about what midterm corrections might be appropriate—and what risks such corrections may entail.

The Institute is publishing this book as a midterm report on the Reagan economic program. The contents are based largely (though not entirely) on two conferences that the Institute cosponsored on Reaganomics with the Claremont Center for the Study of Law Structures. The book is intended as a serious analysis, bringing together economists associated with different ideological perspectives. Some of the authors were broadly sympathetic with the administration's program when it was put in place; others opposed from the beginning its principal features.

We hope that this book will make a significant contribution to the continuing debate on how best to assure the economic prosperity and growth that all of us want.

Glenn S. Dumke
President
Institute for Contemporary Studies

I

Introduction

1

Wm. CRAIG STUBBLEBINE

THOMAS D. WILLETT

The Reagan Program: An Overview

From the earliest days of the Republic, the fates of presidents and parties have been bound up with the performance of the national economy. The era of the New Deal strengthened this link between economics and politics, and the Employment Act of 1946, by mandating a national macroeconomic policy, made it explicit. It is a commonplace of American political life that a president's first duty in the eyes of voters is to deliver prosperity. In the absence of war or other momentous crisis, an administration stands or falls in substantial part on the success of its economic program.

At the same time, in recent years there has been growing recognition of the troubling discrepancy between cycles of political decision making on the one hand and cycles of economic performance on the other. Simply because of the way the economy works, an economic program, once launched, is likely to take a longer time to produce results than voters will be willing to give it. The resulting "political business cycle" has been a major disruptive influence on macroeconomic policymaking in recent times.

At midterm, therefore, the efficacy of an administration's economic program is in principle difficult to evaluate, for both political and economic reasons. For not only are ideological preferences likely to influence one's verdict, but also, at this stage in the process, the economic results are often far from clear-cut.

Understandably, the public at large tends to measure politicians' performance against campaign promises. By this measure, the Reagan program has proved quite unsuccessful in the eyes of some voters—especially in relation to the administration's own bold promises of a "supply-side miracle." Apart from these claims, it is only natural for voters, especially those unschooled in economics, to equate absence of immediate success with failure of the total program.

Yet from a technical standpoint, the failure of the much-touted supply-side experiment is far from the whole story. Even in the earliest days of the administration, faith in the possibility of radical supply-side responses was confined to a tiny minority of economists. Most mainstream economists, whether Keynesian or monetarist, doubted from the outset (to put it mildly) that the administration could achieve immediately and simultaneously all that it set out to achieve: lower taxes, higher defense spending, tighter monetary policy with reduced inflation, and concurrent economic recovery.

The question is, did the supply-side miracle need to work for the administration's overall program to make economic sense? A majority of economists in this volume answer no. Of course, even economists who agree with the administra-

tion's basic strategy will argue about particular details of the
Reagan program. But behind the administration's supply-
side rhetoric has actually been a quite traditional mix of
restrictive fiscal and monetary policies, which many economists—including a number writing here—would argue are
broadly what the economy needs. Against the background of
this more traditional mainstream economic thinking, many
economists would contend that the Reagan program in fact
has strong prospects of long-term success.

According to this more traditional understanding, recovery and disinflation would not occur simultaneously. Rather,
restoration of stable prices and more rapid real growth would
proceed in stages. First, a recession, brought on by lower
rates of monetary growth and lower federal spending, would
dampen the inflation. Then, the positive effects of stable
prices and lower rates of taxation would restore economic
growth and full employment.

In light of this alternative scenario, there are many
hopeful signs. The growth of the money supply has been
restrained, with continuing administration support. If the
costs of the resulting recession have been high in terms of
high interest rates and painful unemployment, they must be
weighed against the long-run costs of continued and rising
inflation. Even after taking into account fortuitous developments, inflation has fallen much more rapidly than most economic analysts, including the administration's, expected. If
this is due in part to a recession deeper than anticipated, the
ratio of temporarily higher unemployment to reductions in
the rate of inflation has been favorable in terms of historical
experience. The inflation fight is being won. Evidence also is
developing that the recession has "bottomed out," that recovery towards full employment is beginning.

As things are working out, national economic policy has
followed and is following a time-tested strategy for restoring
economic stability. That the administration would see itself
as pursuing a "supply-side" program in no way undermines

the coherence or constructive economic validity of the policy combinations effectively being pursued. At worst, it may be said that some of the right things are happening, if for the wrong reasons.

At the same time, implementation of the administration's programs may be open to a number of criticisms. The initial slowdown in the rate of monetary growth may have been too rapid and the volatility of that monetary growth around its decelerating trend may have been too great. Financial innovations and uncertainties about other developments that influence the demand and supply of the various monetary aggregates leave room for considerable differences in judgment among monetary experts.

The excessively rosy administration forecasts, the publicly visible disputes among administration officials and Federal Reserve members as to particular aspects of policy, and the continuing concerns about large budget deficits have lowered the speed with which the public has revised its inflationary expectations. In consequence, interest rates have been slow to respond to the improving outlook for price stability.

Any deficiencies in execution, however, have not been so great as to undermine the basic effort. Inflation has diminished. At this point, to abandon prematurely the policy of monetary restraint, in hopes of promoting quick economic recovery, would be to destroy the costly but necessary investment that has already been made in reversing almost two decades of inflationary excesses. It would leave the economy susceptible to a renewed process of upward ratcheting in the underlying rate of inflation with all of the economic uncertainties, inefficiencies, and inequities this would generate.

Much greater doubts may be expressed about the emerging budget policy. The major problem is not that the current deficit is much too large; the greater part is due to the effects of the current recession. The disturbing feature from an economic perspective is the projection of continuing large deficits even after the economy is recovered. The message of these large deficits is that the various elements of the "politically acceptable" economic program are not fully consistent with one another.

Over the decade ahead, these deficits cannot be justified. Either federal spending must be dramatically reduced, or tax rates must be dramatically increased, or some compromise combination of reduced spending and increased taxes must be achieved. The failure to make significant progress on this issue may reflect a failure to appreciate the magnitudes of the accelerations in federal spending built into current programs. It may reflect an inability of Congress to reconcile constructively pressures to increase spending and to cut taxes. If so, a case may be made for a Constitutional amendment prescribing a balanced budget and tax-spending limitation.

The failure to make progress in balancing federal spending and revenues may reflect overly optimistic supply-side effects. In particular, there appears to have been a failure to distinguish between the moderate supply-side position that not enough attention has been paid to the disincentive effects of government policies and the extreme supply-side argument that tax cuts would "pay for themselves."

One key objective of the Reagan economic program is a dramatic reduction in the burden of federal regulation. Not only has there been basic disagreement about the administration's objective, but some distressing discrepancies between administration promise and actual policies have become evident.

Finally, there continues to be serious controversy over the effects of fiscal restraint on income distribution and poverty levels, in both the short and long run. These issues arouse strong passions on both sides and can be expected to play an important role in the continuing debate over economic policy.

There was and continues to be widespread support for the broad directions of changes in spending, taxing, and regulation advocated by the Reagan administration—that is, slowing down the growth of total federal spending while strengthening defense, reducing federal taxes, eliminating costly regulatory barriers to efficient markets both domestic and international, and realigning relationships between the federal government and the several states.

Progress has been made on all fronts. Nevertheless, key issues remain involving both the magnitudes of these changes and the details of their implementation. In particular, Congress continues to be divided into three minority camps: those who favor dramatic program changes to bring spending down to available revenues, those who favor dramatic changes in the tax laws to bring revenues up to current spending levels, and those who believe the economy requires the continuing stimulation of still more spending and still lower taxes. The result is policy made and executed in fits and starts, ebbing and flowing first in one direction and then in another.

The prospects for the reestablishment of a stable economic environment would be enhanced by a broadly based consensus on economic policy.

II

Inflation, Interest Rates, and Unemployment

2

THOMAS D. WILLETT

Fighting Stagflation: Macroeconomics under Reagan

The history of macroeconomic policymaking and of the performance of the U.S. economy since the mid-1960s makes for a dismal tale.[1] Alternating policies of stimulation and restriction have led to corresponding accelerations and decelerations of inflation, with troughs deepening with each episode. In each instance, restrictive policies have been abandoned before inflation has been subdued. With each round, stagflation has worsened. While some of the poor economic performance of the decade can be ascribed to various adverse shocks from the outside, such as the huge oil price increases in 1973–1974 and again in 1979, most of the history of worsening stagflation can be told in strictly domestic terms. It is against this historical background that the Reagan initiatives should be evaluated.

At the time of President Reagan's election, one could distinguish three prevailing views regarding the proper approach to macroeconomic strategy. Proponents of the first view opposed the traditional medicine of restrictive monetary and fiscal policies. They argued either that such macroeconomic policies would not work (an opinion held mostly by noneconomists), or that even though they would work, the costs in unemployment would be too high (the opinion of many Keynesians). These groups advised either imposing wage and price controls or learning to live with high inflation. A second school, composed of both Keynesians and monetarists, was skeptical that inflation could be stabilized at high levels and believed that the "old-time religion" of restrictive macroeconomic policies was still the correct prescription.[2] These economists acknowledged that a substantial transitional period of high unemployment and economic slack would be required to beat inflation, but they believed that the transition could be relatively short—unlike some Keynesians, who predicted a transition period of high unemployment lasting as long as ten or even twenty years. The president appeared to embrace yet a third view—that with the proper mix of policies, inflation could be subdued and growth could be stimulated simultaneously and painlessly. This new brew of economic medicine combined the magic of supply-side tax cuts with elements of "rational-expectations" economics and monetarism.

Few mainstream economists were surprised when the president's rosy scenario failed to come to pass. Even at the time, many economists criticized the administration's optimistic initial projections, which were based on suppositions inconsistent with historical experience. Yet now that such skepticism has been confirmed, it is worth asking precisely where the administration has succeeded and failed in its macroeconomic strategy, and what options remain open to it for the immediate future.

The Credibility Issue

The problems faced by the administration have been as much rhetorical as economic, and in reviewing its performance, it is important to keep the rhetorical issues distinct from issues of substance. For example, criticism by numerous economists of the administration's overly optimistic *forecasting* should not be confused with opposition to the basic direction of economic policy. It is likely that the substantial portion of economists in the "mainstream" category still favor the basic strategy of tax and spending cuts and reductions in the rate of monetary expansion. Yet even economists sympathetic to the basic thrust of the policy could easily have reservations about its actual implementation.

At the heart of the issue has been the question of credibility. It is ironic that an administration so apparently receptive to recognizing the economic importance of expectations—as emphasized by the recent rational-expectations revolution in economic theory—should have damaged its own credibility in the beginning by resting its policy on implausible forecasts. With regard to rhetorical strategy, the administration would have been better advised to acknowledge frankly that reducing inflation would require pain and to prepare the public for it. Such a rhetorical stance would have left the total economic program in a more credible position today.

In the wake of the recession, the administration's rhetoric has grown more realistic. Still, gains on this score have been offset by other factors. Public quarreling between administration officials and the Federal Reserve over the blame for high interest rates did little to instill confidence in financial markets. This bickering with the Federal Reserve, combined with the intramural dispute in the administration between monetarists and supply-siders, contributed for a long time to an impression of disarray. The president's apparent reluctance to take action on the deficit, despite the reported pressure from his own economic advisors, added to the appearance of confusion. The 1982 tax increase and expenditure reduction package was very late in coming, but it did represent an important step in bringing the deficit under control.

The key issue left open in the wake of the tax increase debate is not the size of the budget deficit over the coming year, but the future credibility of the president's overall strategy. It is important to recognize that a substantial proportion of this year's budget deficit will be due to the recession. Estimates for the so-called "full-employment deficit," which cancel out the effects of recession, now hover around 1 to 1.5 percent of GNP. This is higher than optimal, but it can plausibly be argued that such a deficit is not so large as to place severe pressures on the Federal Reserve for monetary accommodation or to generate massive "crowding out" of private investment. With regard to arguments against the tax increase itself, there is certainly merit in the contention that the middle of a recession is not a good time for tax increases (even if they are only partially offsetting scheduled tax decreases).[3] What is particularly worrisome, however, is the longer-run budget outlook. The administration's projections have shown continuing large (although falling) deficits. The projections of the Congressional Budget Office (CBO) have been less optimistic, predicting that deficits will be substantially larger. For FY 1985, the CBO forecast was almost double the administration's projections. Typically, the projections of independent analysts have come much closer to those of the CBO than to those of the administration.

The truth seems to be that once one gives up the hope for supply-side responses far outside the range of historical experience, it is difficult to avoid the view that the president's major goals—incremental tax cuts, a buildup in military spending—are incompatible with the elimination of the budget deficit over the next several years, especially given realistic forecasts of additional cutbacks in domestic spending likely to pass Congress. Even in the early days of the program, typical nonadministration projections foresaw full-employment budget deficits rising rapidly from around 1 percent of GNP in fiscal year 1982 to between 3 and 5 percent in 1985.

Effects of Deficits

It seems likely that such deficits will develop. If so, will they have disastrous effects on the economy, destroying any chance to cure inflation and restore steady economic growth? The answer is probably no. There has been a good deal of recent discussion of the extent to which budget deficits are inflationary and/or crowd out private investment. On this issue it is crucial to distinguish between full-employment deficits and those caused primarily by recession. The latter would be expected to place less pressure on interest rates and are less likely to stimulate monetary accommodation or substantial crowding out of private investment. My own empirical work suggests that in the past, full-employment deficits have stimulated substantial amounts of monetary accommodation.[4] That does not necessarily imply that it will occur again in the current situation, especially in the wake of the October 1979 change in Federal Reserve policy that targets monetary aggregates rather than interest rates as policy indicators. In fact, the press reports give the impression that at present the Federal Reserve is very concerned *not* to let higher budget deficits generate monetary accommodation, so much so that the Fed has seemed at times unwilling to ease monetary policy unless the budget deficits were scaled down. Of course, there is still the problem that the Federal Reserve's actions have by no means always conformed to its announced policy intentions; many observers are less than fully convinced about the likely endurance of the Federal Reserve's current laudable resolve. Nonetheless, while large budget deficits will undoubtedly make the Federal Reserve's job much more difficult, and slow the speed with which inflationary expectations are reduced, they will not necessarily cause a higher price level over the long run. If the Federal Reserve were to remain on a firm course of gradually reducing the average rate of monetary expansion to a noninflationary level, then the major effect of deficits would be higher real interest rates and relatively lower rates of private investment. In the short run, meanwhile, industries such as housing and autos are bound to be particularly hard hit by tighter credit conditions.

As with the question of monetary accommodation, the effects of budget deficits on crowding out of private investment will depend crucially on the cause of the deficit. If the deficit is caused primarily by a recession, then there is likely to be little crowding out, and stimulative fiscal policy could even cause an increase in private investment (traditional Keynesian "pump priming"). Likewise, a deficit generated by tax breaks for investment may have substantial net stimulative effects on investment, even if the deficit portion of the policy does itself cause considerable crowding out. On the other hand, general reductions in income taxes unaccompanied by government expenditure reductions are likely to lead to net crowding out of private investment. To prevent this, one would need to have either very substantial short-run Keynesian stimulative effects on aggregate demand (possible only in an economy with a great deal of economic slack) or huge supply-side effects that greatly increase the level of full-employment output. The administration has put great stress on boosting savings as a way of countering crowding out. But at full employment, general tax cuts are bound on balance to cause crowding out unless the marginal propensity to save is 1—i.e., unless there is no increase in private consumption—which is unlikely. Thus even with the very high savings responses predicted by the administration (much greater than those projected by most private forecasters), the tax cuts will inevitably lead to some crowding out at a constant level of output.

Two other points should be raised about the potential adverse effects of large budget deficits. One is that popular arguments that the large budget deficits will strangle the economic recovery do not find support in conventional economic theory. Under strong monetarist assumptions the net effect of the budget deficit should be expansionary or at most neutral with regard to growth. A deficit will not have a net deflationary effect except insofar as it might adversely affect expectations, as will be discussed below. A second point is that the optimal long-run full-employment budget deficit is not necessarily zero (i.e., a balanced budget). Indeed, a very good case can be made that one of the best ways to stimulate private investment and increase productivity over the longer run may be to run budget surpluses, thus adding to the net savings of the economy.

Deficits and Credibility

Potentially one of the most damaging aspects of the large current and projected future deficits has been the extent to which they have raised doubts about the credibility of the administration's commitment to ending inflation. Initially the apparent unwillingness of the president to adjust major elements of his game plan in response to such projections fueled doubts both about his understanding of the economic trade-offs likely to be involved and about his willingness to carry through on his anti-inflation pledges, especially as it became increasingly clear that achieving his goals would involve considerable pain. As Herbert Stein put it before the president endorsed the need for tax increases, "Mr. Reagan continues to say that balancing the budget is important. But if he is unwilling to sacrifice anything of importance to him in order to balance the budget, others will hardly believe that he takes the goal very seriously or that they should do so."[5] The rationales given by the president in his State of the Union message for opposing tax increases were likewise unlikely to increase his credibility with the economic and financial communities. The president stated boldly that "higher taxes would not mean lower deficits," citing evidence not really relevant to the policy change under debate. He also argued that raising taxes "will encourage more government spending and less private investment." While the first half of this claim is quite plausible, albeit arguable, the latter part would be true only if tax increases were skewed toward investment. The taxes under discussion were definitely not of this type.

Even in the absence of such rhetorical inaccuracies, it would be understandable for the business and financial communities to entertain doubts about the sustainability of anti-inflation efforts, given the poor performance of previous administrations in this regard. After all, one could hardly have boasted better political credentials than Richard Nixon's for getting tough on inflation, and yet even Nixon fell victim to the collision between long-term economic and short-term political goals. The pattern has been apparent over and over again: just as administrations are tempted into overly expansionary policies because the benefits of temporarily higher output tend to be concentrated before the costs of high inflation, so they are pressured into premature abandonment of anti-inflationary measures because the costs in temporarily higher unemployment tend to be felt much more quickly than the benefits of slower inflation. The latter was the case with Nixon in 1971. Impatience over the rate at which inflation was slowing, and the prospect of running for reelection with a slack economy, induced a dramatic switch in policy in midcourse. The economy was restimulated well before the battle against inflation had been won.

Until he decided to support the recent tax measure, President Reagan had done little to reassure the economy that under similar circumstances he would behave differently. His initial reactions to the failure of his rosy forecasts, the imprecision of his policy statements, the public criticism of the Federal Reserve—none of this helped to instill confidence that the administration would hold to its basic anti-inflationary course.

From a purely economic standpoint, it is quite clear that in their commitment to gradual disinflation the administration and the Federal Reserve are pursuing a sound strategy. At the same time, by its reliance on overly optimistic projects and its hesitance to acknowledge apparent contradictions in its economic program, the administration has also damaged its credibility substantially. What is important to recognize is that this loss of credibility has concrete economic effects.

As is now well understood, the greater the general concern about the credibility of anti-inflationary objectives, the longer it will take to end inflation and the greater will be the transitional costs of unemployment and lost output that will be generated.

The recent well-publicized "accord" between the Federal Reserve and the administration is certainly a useful step toward improving credibility. Likewise, the president's support of a tax increase and its successful navigation through Congress have also increased confidence. These developments were not the sole cause of the substantial decline in interest rates over the summer of 1982, but they played an important role.

The 1982 budget legislation, however, is not enough to bring future budget deficits under control. It will be necessary to find additional means of enhancing the credibility of both the administration's and the Fed's commitment to ending inflation. On the fiscal policy side, obvious possibilities include further scaling back or slowing down of the projected rate of growth of military spending, and the adoption of institutional reforms such as the balanced budget amendment that increase the prospects of substantial further cuts in domestic government spending. These and other possibilities need to be debated in terms of both their desirability and their likely credibility.[6]

With respect to monetary policy, an obvious point stressed in the recent report of the Council of Economic Advisers is that a steadier rate of monetary growth would help stabilize expectations about Federal Reserve intentions. It has been argued, in fact, that the variability in the rate of monetary growth—as distinct from the size of the rate—has actually been a major contribution to high interest rates. During 1981, however, it was difficult to see how monetary growth rates could be stabilized. Not only were there numerous in-stances of instability—giving rise to substantial disagree-ment between Keynesians and monetarists as to the relative importance of interest rates versus monetary aggregates at a particular point in time—but the various financial innova-tions and changes in banking regulation also provoked sub-stantial differences of opinion among monetarists concern-ing the relative importance of the major monetary aggre-gates (M_1, M_2, etc.). Unfortunately, moreover, the various major aggregates at times give radically different signals about the course of policy. Thus our discussion of these issues needs to go well beyond the question of whether or not a money growth rule should be adopted.

The Most Desirable Time Path for Disinflation

Another major policy question concerns the appropriate time to begin restimulation of the economy. Obviously we would like to end inflation at the lowest possible cost. We do not want to subject the economy to a longer and more severe period of economic slack than necessary. Unfortunately, however, we cannot predict the behavior of the economy with sufficient precision to be confident in selecting the minimum cost path. Thus it becomes important to weigh the relative net costs of erring on the side of too much or too little cumulative restraint. A strong case can be made for erring on the side of maintaining restraint for too long rather than too short a period. As noted above, in the process of gradual disinflation the ratio of current costs to benefits is initially quite high but declines substantially over time. By reversing policy too soon, one will have faced a much higher proportion of the total costs of disinflation than of the total benefits. The declining ratio of marginal costs to benefits until disinflation is complete means that the net cost of removing disinflationary policies a month too soon will be greater than that of keeping them for a month too long (assuming, of course, that the total cost-benefit ratios are such that the disinflationary strategy made sense in the first place).

In addition, given the recent history of premature abandonments of anti-inflation efforts, it seems likely that people are conditioned to expect such behavior. Consequently, expansionary policies are likely to shift up inflationary expectations more rapidly than contractionary policies will reduce them. Under these circumstances, the premature abandonment of restrictive policy would not only directly rekindle inflationary pressures, but would also make the next anti-inflation effort even more difficult.

The difficulty of choosing the most desirable time path is exacerbated by the disagreement among economists about the inflationary effects of economic expansion while considerable slack remains in the economy. There is fairly widespread agreement that President Nixon's post-1971 expansionary policies were primarily motivated by short-run political goals. In contrast, the adoption of more expansionary policies toward the beginning of President Carter's term reflected the (controversial) view that as long as a margin of unused resources remained, expansionary policies could be adopted without severely interfering with continued reduction of inflation. On the other hand, many monetarists feared that such a restimulation would worsen inflation, and

eclectic researchers like Robert Gordon found evidence that
the rate of change of economic slack, as well as its level, had
powerful effects on wage and price behavior.[7]

While we have many instances of accelerating output and
falling inflation over short periods of time, the available
econometric evidence raises serious doubts about this
possibility over the medium term. The clarity of the Carter
experiment was confounded by serious supply shocks that
contributed to the subsequent increase in inflation, but the
episode does not give grounds for optimism that a substantial
acceleration would not have occurred in any event. In this
connection, one can hope that the current administration's
projections of the speed of recovery are in fact too optimistic—as they have been widely judged.

Because of the need to establish credibility over time, the
optimal method for curing inflation (as contrasted with
hyperinflation, where shock treatment is likely to be needed)
is probably mild substantial restraint designed to minimize
the conflicting inflationary pressures generated by rapid
growth from high levels of slack.[8] *From this perspective, the
current recession has probably been more severe than would
be optimal, but this does not necessarily mean that we can
compensate for it by trying to engineer a more rapid recovery.*

The most desirable course of monetary and fiscal policy
over the coming year needs to be considered carefully with
this problem in mind. These concerns should make one
especially wary of adopting proposals for a considerably more
expansionary monetary policy in order to reduce real interest rates, even if one believes that more rapid monetary
expansion can lower real interest rates over any sustained
period of time—a proposition that is, at best, controversial.[9]

International Aspects

Another set of questions concerns the international aspects
of U.S. stabilization policy. On the favorable side, it has been

argued that sizeable international capital inflows induced by high U.S. interest rates can contribute to reducing substantially the amount of crowding out of domestic private investment generated by budget deficits. Likewise, the sharp appreciation of the dollar from mid-1980 through mid-1981 by over 20 percent on a trade-weighted basis (in both nominal and real terms) has probably contributed notably in the short run to the reduction in the inflation rate.

This tends to confirm a point that has been emphasized recently by a number of international economists—namely, that (contrary to the frequent charges that floating exchange rates are a major contributor to inflationary problems) flexible exchange rates are likely to make anti-inflationary policies easier to implement.[10] By speeding up price changes, flexible rates tend to intensify short-run inflation/unemployment trade-offs. While much has been made of how this can worsen the inflationary problems of countries following expansionary policies, the relationship is symmetrical, and consequently countries following anti-inflationary policies find that the deceleration of inflation is also speeded up.

The international aspects of U.S. financial policies have also been the subject of considerable criticism, however. From a domestic perspective, critics such as former Assistant Secretary of the Treasury C. Fred Bergsten have charged that U.S. macroeconomic policies, in combination with tendencies for overreaction in the foreign exchange market and the current U.S. policy of foregoing official intervention (except in cases of extremely disorderly markets), have led to a considerable overvaluation of the dollar. This overvaluation, it is argued, is currently retarding economic growth, and the future anticipated downward plunge of the dollar will then substantially worsen domestic inflationary conditions.[11] There has also been widely expressed concern abroad that high U.S. interest rates and the strong dollar are strangling worldwide economic recovery.

Such concerns are legitimate, although the weight of recent research suggests that they tend to be considerably overstated.[12] Moreover, the record of effectiveness of heavy official management of exchange rates by the industrial countries to reduce volatility does not give one great cause for optimism that more substantial official intervention in the exchange markets can be a major source of increased stability.

In retrospect, one can certainly argue that a somewhat smaller appreciation of the dollar would have been preferable, especially as in recent months the dollar has fallen back to some degree. However, it is not at all clear that the dollar has become substantially overvalued. Charges that this is so typically rely on comparisons with various Purchasing Power Parity calculations (based on differences in national inflation rates). Recent theoretical and empirical research has shown rather conclusively, however, that these are extremely poor guides to the estimation of equilibrium exchange rates.

There can be little question that the strengthening of the dollar has in a number of instances created increased short-run difficulties abroad. Although empirical research generally finds considerably less macroeconomic interdependence among nations than is implied in many popular discussions and political complaints, such effects are not wholly negligible. Yet it should be pointed out that just as foreign countries are now sharing the costs of our disinflationary policies, they will likewise share the benefits of a more stable economic environment if, in fact, these efforts are carried through to success.

Institutional Reforms

Are there major institutional reforms capable of forestalling the types of policy mistakes that culminated in the vicious stagflation inherited by the current administration? It should be said at the outset that the two most straightforward proposals—a return to some form of substantive gold standard and a constitutionally mandated simple monetary growth rule—have serious disadvantages.

A gold standard could subject the economy to both long-run trends and short-run fluctuations in monetary expansion that would be entirely inappropriate to the needs of the domestic economy. Similarly, a constitutionally mandated monetary rule (fixing monetary growth at a certain constant level) would be dangerously insensitive to the variations in velocity that accompany innovations in financial practice. The notion of a monetary rule is also rendered problematic by our uncertainty about the best ways to define money.[13]

There are other institutional reforms to be considered. One could, for example, remove the independence of the Federal Reserve and make monetary policy the direct responsibility of the president.[14] In this way the electorate could legitimately hold the president and Congress directly responsible for macroeconomic policy. Such a measure would also eliminate the pattern of mutual recriminations between the Federal Reserve and the administration. Yet even with its current independence, the Federal Reserve has not been perfectly insulated from political pressure, and it is not at all clear that such a change would be sufficient to end the "political business cycle." The public has of course over time become more aware of the tendencies to stimulate the economy for political purposes. This should reduce the incentives for such behavior, but how meaningful this effect will be is open to considerable question. The typical voter may have little incentive to be sufficiently informed on macroeconomic issues. Thus it seems that some type of constraint on the scope for discretionary macroeconomic policies is likely to be necessary.

Perhaps most attractive would be a two-part strategy in which the Fed's target outcomes would be expressed in terms of average rates of growth of nominal income, and the law would require that violations of the target ranges be corrected by adjustments in the rate of growth of M_1 or some other monetary aggregate. (Corresponding corrections to fiscal policy might be required as well.) Such approaches need to be considered carefully, however, in terms of both economic content and appropriate forms of political implementation. It would be beneficial if the recent public and congressional interest in the possible return to a gold standard and in balanced budget amendments were to be broadened into a major examination of these issues,[15] but I do not think we should rush hastily into the adoption of a set of rules that we might soon find to be inappropriate. This would only end up further reducing the credibility of government economic policymaking.

RESPONSES

William H. Branson: "The Problem
Is Not Credibility"

The Reagan administration inherited an economy that was suffering from low growth rates of both productivity and real income, and from a subsequent stagflation. The administration's stabilization policy package raised both long-term and short-term real interest rates: the attempt to lock in a long-run easy fiscal policy pushed up long-term interest rates, and the tight monetary policy with a focus on growth rates of aggregates alone pushed up short-term interest rates. The effects were transmitted abroad by high real rates that contributed to recessions in Europe and Japan. This combination of an easy fiscal policy and a tight monetary policy will choke off investment and exacerbate the productivity problem.

Thus I don't think that the basic problem is one of credibility, as Professor Willett's paper seems to imply. I think one has to be seen as having the economic analysis right to be credible. The markets understand what's happening; that's why real rates are so high. By sticking to the supply-side religion and simple monetary growth rules, the administration got the economic analysis wrong, and that has made establishing credibility difficult.

There has been a major slowdown in real growth of productivity and real income all over the industrial world. The fact that this slowdown has been international would lead me to disagree with Willett's statement that one can find the roots of U.S. policy problems in domestic sources. The productivity slowdown has caused a cost-push pressure and stagflation. People made decisions about things like buying homes or automobiles or educating children on the implicit assumption that their real incomes would grow by 3.2 percent a year—a figure virtually etched in stone by the Kennedy administration Council of Economic Advisers. Suddenly they found that real income was growing on an average of zero percent a year and they were surprised and frustrated in their real consumption plans. Their reaction has been to push up whatever wage and price they have any control over. That creates a cost-push pressure in the economy. In this situation, the last thing one wants to do is adopt a stabilization program that raises real interest rates and reduces investment.

I agree with Willett's points about the deficit. The problem is not in the short run with the recession but with the fact that the administration's projections and the CBO's projections show substantial deficits at full employment in the 1980s. These deficits themselves raise questions about whether or not the economy will reach those full-employment paths, but let us take it as given that it's possible.

The large deficit at full employment implies a monetary policy that is tight enough to reduce the ratio of private investment to GNP sufficiently to make room for financing the deficit out of saving. Monetary policy will have to be tight enough to make real interest rates high enough to squeeze down investment, making room for that deficit. It's hard to predict how high real interest rates would have to be to do that, but the market seems to think that 8 percent or so in terms of long-term real interest rates will do it.

The sources of the problem of high real interest rates are the multi-year tax cut based on supply-side thinking and the increases in defense expenditures. This is a stabilization policy mistake that is at least partially due to the supply-side religion. The other stabilization mistake that I would cite is a focus solely on money growth rates, which has raised short-term real interest rates.

Consider a Federal Reserve policy of tightening the growth rate of some set of monetary aggregates until inflation subsides, and suppose that the policy is sufficiently credible that it reduces the current expected rate of inflation. Now Milton Friedman taught us in his restatement of the quantity theory of money that the demand for money depends on the expected rate of inflation. The argument there was basically that the expected rate of inflation is the margin of substitution between money and durable goods. Thus, if there is an increase in the expected rate of inflation, people tend to get out of money-fixed assets and into durable goods. But on the other side of the coin, if there is a substantial reduction in the expected rate of inflation, people get out of durable goods and back into money. So a fall in the expected rate of inflation, which would follow from a credible Fed policy of steady reduction in money growth, tends to shift up the demand for money now. That tends to raise equilibrium short-term interest rates relative to the current rate of inflation, which means an increase in short-term real rates.

If the Fed follows growth rate rules alone, it cannot accommodate shifts in money demand that come from shifts in inflationary expectations generated by the Fed's following the growth rate rules. So simply reducing the money growth rate and sticking to it eventually reduces the expected rate of inflation. At that point, money demand shifts up. The Fed is trapped because it cannot accommodate that upward shift without seeming to have given up on the growth rate target, and real interest rates go up at the short end. While this in a sense is a problem for the Fed rather than for the Reagan administration, it comes from the simple policy prescription urged by administration officials of looking only at monetary growth rates—against the sensible resistance of the Fed.

Beryl W. Sprinkel: "Internal Consistency of the Reagan Program"

As economists, we are acutely aware of our infirmity of two-handedness. My own particular condition is further aggravated by the fact that these days I appear on discussion panels as a two-headed monster: a government official, expected to supply a vigorous defense of administration policies; and a professional economist, expected to contribute to a lively, scholarly debate. As many of you who have held visible government positions know, wearing two hats may cause an occasional headache. So in order to avoid this eventuality, my two bowlers have just merged into one sombrero, and I do not have to fear any longer of developing a personality split. I'll just be me. To a great extent, I owe my salvation to Tom Willett, who in his appraisal of this administration's policies took proper care in distinguishing among theory, evidence, forecasts, political pronouncements, value judgments, and personal opinions. Such a careful distinction among sources of criticism of any economic program is, in my judgment, a desirable and necessary precondition for an intelligent discussion of pertinent issues.

With regard to the Reagan program, one must take a close look at the problem of its internal consistency. I must humbly admit that, from the standpoint of economic theory, it's not at all that novel. It is rather a combination of various stands of neoclassical economics.

What does the program imply about the assignment of policy instruments?

First, monetary policy is assigned the task of stabilizing the price level. This assignment has implications for exchange rates, interest rates, and other variables, but essentially it points at prices.

Second, the secular trend of government expenditures is determined by the perceived necessary supply of goods of collective consumption, and by various contractual obligations that can't get changed.

Third, the tax structure is assigned the role of minimizing impediments to production and investment. The choice between funding the government at the margin by taxation or by borrowing is determined by the time preference between present and future consumption. Consequently, the budget deficit is determined by the level of necessary government expenditures and the degree of its reluctance to borrow.

Fourth, the determination of the level of unemployment is left to management and labor. In an open economy, there is a trade-off between higher real wages and higher unemployment.

Finally, the task of maintaining external balance is assigned to flexible exchange rates.

As long as the budget deficit is not treated as an exogenous constraint, I would be quite confident to contend that the theoretical model underlying the president's program displays perfect internal consistency.

Let us try now to put some meat on this theoretical skeleton. There are a few distinct sets of issues that need to be addressed. I will dispose of them at once, not because they are unimportant but rather because they could take our discussion too far afield. One is the role of government in the society. People can argue endlessly about the appropriate level and composition of government expenditures, and we do. I do confess that I think we are allocating too many resources to government, and the sooner we cut that allocation, the more efficient our economy will be. And I won't talk about the political environment—it is too easy to forget that enacted tax and spending bills are quite different from the original wishes of any administration, including our own. I would urge, therefore, some circumspection in assessing the administration's ability to shape its economic policy exactly as it would like to do. We can propose; we certainly cannot— alone—dispose.

With these caveats in mind, I'd like to return to some critical points regarding the matter of consistency that Tom Willett raises in his paper.

Is our fiscal policy too loose?

The president thinks so. And so do I. And he recommends further cuts in spending. His critics, apparently, agree with him on the question of looseness but would like to remedy the situation by raising revenues. These are questions falling as much within the domain of one's political philosophy as within that of economic theory. We have to be honest about the terms of the ongoing discourse.

Herb Stein, for instance, is quoted by Tom Willett as saying that the president is apparently "unwilling to sacrifice anything of importance to him in order to balance the budget"; simultaneously, as a member of the Committee on the Present Danger, Stein calls for a substantial increase of military spending above what the president proposed. Would Herb Stein be happy if the president, in order to balance the budget, sacrificed something of importance to him—namely, an increase in funding of the nation's defense? Analogous questions can be addressed to other critics of the looseness of our fiscal policy. Furthermore, we believe that higher taxes, on balance, will lead not to a balanced budget but to further spending increases.

Another question relates to monetary policy. Is it too tight?

By choosing our criteria creatively, one can always show this to be the case. There is a great tendency to argue in favor of easier money. Some critics would point toward high inflation-adjusted short-term interest rates, others towards the so-called overvaluation of the dollar relative to other major currencies. Others, still, would invoke the drop in real economic activity, while still another group of critics would look at the rate of growth of total credit, rather than at a narrow measure of money. Personally, I think that as long as the rate of growth of M_1 exceeds the rate of growth of total output by a few percentage points, the case for monetary policy's being too tight cannot be convincingly made.

Essentially, however, as Willett properly points out, the argument comes down to the question of what is the optimal path of disinflation. And that's a very difficult question— one that we did, in fact, wrestle with a great deal, early on in this administration. We opted for what we referred to as gradualism, not cold turkey.

We stated, if you may remember, that it was our hope that we could reduce the rate of growth in the money supply by half in the next four years, and we referred here to either M_1 or the base. In fact, we got 75 percent of that adjustment last year. And clearly, we also got a much sharper contraction in economic activity and inflation rates than we had bargained for.

Even the most severe critics acknowledge that this administration has achieved a remarkable reduction in the rate of inflation. I give credit for that accomplishment partly to the administration but in considerable amount to the Federal Reserve, even though it has been tighter, on average, than we wanted.

No one would deny that this disinflation of the economy resulted in considerable discomfort to millions of individuals. Would a somewhat less restrictive monetary policy have resulted in a lesser present net discounted value of aggregate pain over time? My guess is that it would have, but clearly the direction of the monetary targets chosen has the complete endorsement of this administration.

One of the messages contained in Willett's paper is that an economic program, even if consistent, need not necessarily be credible. I would like to devote a few minutes to this problem. It is important to distinguish between the credibility of intentions and the credibility of outcomes.

Even granted that I'm not an unbiased judge of this administration's determination to stick to its announced economic policies, given our record I sometimes wonder what it does

take to earn one's badge of trustworthiness. As we had promised, we reduced the growth of hundreds of government
spending programs well beyond what before 4 November
1980 was universally considered politically possible.

We eliminated a great many shackling regulations, and
are continuing on that front. We refrained from intervening
in foreign exchange markets. We haven't resorted to bail-
outs of shaky enterprises. We didn't buckle under to the
threat of a potentially crippling strike by a public employees'
union, and so on and so on.

Significantly, in the midst of a rather severe recession—in
a midterm election year—we have not attempted to pressure
the Federal Reserve to expand the money supply more
rapidly. Can there still be any doubt regarding this administration's commitment to its economic policy? I think not.

I do recognize, however, that even among those people who
believe in the Reagan administration's ability to persevere in
pursuing its policies, many doubt that these policies will yield
the promised results. That is what I call the credibility of outcomes. The expressed doubts center around the presumed
crowding-out phenomenon during the recovery phase.

As the story goes, high real cost of credit will discourage
investment and nip the recovery in the bud. In order to stave
off this calamity, a reduction in the government borrowing
requirement by means of raising taxes is being widely suggested. And since the administration is demonstrably resis-
tant to the idea of raising taxes, its economic forecast of
resumed sustainable growth is not to be believed.

Neither the above scenario of continued sluggishness in
the economy nor the cure proposed by administration critics
seems entirely plausible to me.

To begin with, the odds are overwhelming that inflation-
adjusted long-term interest rates will come down substantially. Their present level simply cannot be sustained much
longer at present and prospective rates of inflation.

Granted, a reduction in the government deficit, other

things remaining the same, would depress those long-term real rates even further. But how relevant is this observation if the reduction is to be achieved by raising taxes? Is it clear that the cure is better than the disease? One must pause before advocating raising taxes. If government expenditures increase to the full extent of the incremental tax increase, the case against this course of action is clear-cut and requires no further elaboration. But if every additional dollar in tax increases should generate, say, only 50 cents in additional spending, the government would still be preempting a larger share of the nation's resources than under present proposals. I doubt that this would stimulate a burst of economic activity. Certainly not in the longer run.

Furthermore, I do not share the confidence that a reduction in federal deficits, by means of raising taxes, will translate to any appreciable extent into lower real long-term interest rates.

In fact, rescinding the scheduled cut in marginal income taxes may well have the opposite effect. It's worth pointing out that a marginal propensity to save, of less than 1, is a necessary, not a sufficient, condition for reducing the supply of private credit by a lesser amount than the reduction in the government demand for credit due to higher tax revenues.

Should the 10 percent reduction in personal income tax rates scheduled for 1983 be repealed, I would not have to stretch my imagination to conceive that a combination of reduced incentives to work and save, coupled with an incremental increase in government spending, may well lead to higher, not lower, real long-term interest rates.

Finally, I cannot suppress the urge to remind my Keynesian friends that the interest rate or cost of capital services is not the only variable in the standard investment function. In case they have forgotten, expected demand for output figures in this function quite prominently; increasing people's taxes can only depress the expected level of sales and consequently depress today's demand for investment goods.

In sum, I agree wholeheartedly with Tom Willett that at the dawn of this administration we presented projections that were overoptimistic; certainly, we did not factor in the severe recession that we have, and as a result we suffered for a while the pain from both self-inflicted and Fed-inflicted wounds.

I believe, however, that we learned the lesson. We're mending our ways and have come up with a feasible long-term plan of economic revival for our country, and further progress will be evident in the weeks immediately ahead. Most certainly, we have the sense of purpose and the strength of conviction required to secure its implementation.

Jacob Dreyer: "Some International Aspects of U.S. Macroeconomic Policy"

The most frequent criticism levied currently by foreign commentators against the Reagan administration's macroeconomic policies is well known: a mix of tight monetary and loose fiscal policies results in high U.S. interest rates that in turn suck in capital from abroad. As a consequence, foreign governments are faced with a dilemma: either they allow their currencies to weaken vis-à-vis the dollar or they intervene in foreign exchange markets and simultaneously take steps toward restraining domestic credit expansion. In the first case, it is said, they would have to accept the resulting deterioration in their terms of trade; in the second case, they would supposedly experience the depressing consequences of higher domestic interest rates. It is no secret that the U.S. government has been under considerable pressure from its allies to remedy this situation.

What is our reaction to this criticism? The question is to what extent U.S. policies are responsible for the difficulties experienced by foreign economies and what we can or should do to ease these difficulties.

The more thoughtful foreign critics acknowledge that the impact of high U.S. interest rates on their economies has been vastly exaggerated. Conditions and policies in individual countries have an incomparably greater impact on their respective nominal interest rates than anything that happens in the U.S. It is not by chance that nominal interest rates are currently very high in Italy and France, moderately high in Germany and Holland, and low in Japan and Switzerland. More fundamentally, given a very high degree of international capital mobility, one would expect that capital inflows into the United States would tend to depress inflation-adjusted interest rates in the U.S. relative to those abroad. Since this is patently not the case, the explanation must lie elsewhere.

The truth of the matter is that inflation-adjusted rates are high everywhere, with a tendency to be higher in those countries, such as the U.S., that are going through a period of rapid disinflation —as one would expect. The reason for the universally high level of inflation-adjusted interest rates is that the demand for real credit by public authorities is excessive in all industrial countries. Whether or not the U.S. should be declared the main culprit would depend on the definition and measurement of public "excess" demand for credit; and given that it is a worldwide phenomenon, the only way the United States could be singled out for particular blame would simply be because the absolute magnitude of the U.S. government's claims on the pool of savings potentially available in international financial markets is much larger than the magnitude of claims of any other government. High interest rates in the U.S., just as high interest rates in Britain, Belgium, and so on, are due to some extent to inordinately large borrowing requirements of, say, the Italian government, the French government, and many other governments.

The second part of the question is: can and should the U.S. authorities do something to weaken the U.S. contribution to the problem of high interest rates worldwide? There is no conflict between the U.S. and its allies regarding the *goal* of lower interest rates. The conflict arises with respect to the method to be employed to bring interest rates down and the speed with which it is to be accomplished. Simplifying the matter to some extent, one can say that foreign authorities would like us not only to reduce the government borrowing requirements but also to ease our monetary policy. Apart from the question of the desirability of easing on money at the present juncture, it is doubtful that it would have a *lasting* beneficial effect on interest rates. In fact, the chances are that it would produce a perverse effect—that is, it could raise interest rates, especially on long-term instruments. In a nutshell, then, the fundamental conflict between the Europeans and ourselves can be explained by the difference in perceptions of what U.S. monetary policy can accomplish in the current environment. Only after this gap in perception is closed or narrowed would it make sense to talk about differences of views on the desirable time path of disinflation in the U.S. as it affects foreign economies.

A related foreign criticism of U.S. policies is focused more narrowly on our approach to foreign exchange markets. The frequently heard accusations of "benign neglect" imply that as a result of our essentially "hands-off" attitude we are gaining something at the expense of others and neglecting an opportunity to influence events. Neither is true.

We have two basic reasons, and a number of derived ones, for our minimal-intervention policy. The first is our skepticism that any government is capable of second-guessing what the sustainable level of an exchange rate is; the second is that, historically, attempts to fix or manage dollar exchange rates have been spectacularly unsuccessful.

Our reluctance to engage in exchange market intervention, be it unilateral or concerted, does not mean that we are opposed to international economic cooperation. However, because not all policy areas and objectives are equally amenable to cooperation, we believe that efforts at international policy coordination ought to be selective and circumscribed. Since the willingness of individual governments to coordinate their policies is limited, and since the process of coordination can be easily overburdened and bureaucratized, it makes sense to distinguish those policy areas in which international coordination is imperative from those in which it is superfluous and inefficient.

There is little point in trying to coordinate policies that have primarily domestic impacts. For example, an incentive-oriented reform of the tax structure will increase full-employment output at home without directly affecting output abroad. Nevertheless, there remains an important distinction between policies undertaken primarily for the purpose of influencing the external sector (exchange rate management, import surcharges, etc.) and policies that are directed at achieving national aims but that also produce international spillovers as a result of countries' market interdependence. Regarding the former set of policies, carefully designed and limited international cooperation can make itself felt; regarding the latter set, coordination has proved itself to exert very weak influence on the formulation of national policies.

Some national policy instruments are by their nature competitive in character: benefits derived from their application by one country are (in reality or in appearance) matched by costs to be borne by its partners. The most obvious examples of such policy instruments are protective trade practices.

It is clear that use of these policies, if unchecked, is certain to result in enormous damage to the whole community of nations. Yet voluntary restraint on their use by some countries, if unmatched by others, would be correctly viewed as a blatantly inequitable and thus unsustainable situation. Consequently, the case for international coordination of competitive policies is overwhelming. Since close coordination, in fact harmonization, of such policies has the potential for yielding a very substantial collective benefit, national energies and efforts devoted to international cooperation should be channeled toward dealing with inherently competitive national policies.

While the competitiveness of policies mentioned above arises from both their *intent* and their *effect*, the competitiveness of other policies is determined by their perceived intent rather than their outcome. The most obvious example of such a policy instrument is exchange rate management.

Active exchange rate management may be viewed as provocative—potentially competitive and possibly damaging to other countries. In our view, the best way to prevent suspicions of malevolent intent from taking hold is to refrain from active exchange rate management—period. We easily recognize, however, that if other countries find it necessary to actively manage their exchange rates, a coordinated approach à la EMS is vastly preferable to an uncoordinated one.

In short, a deficient performance in policy by some nations negates or reduces the efforts of the others. However, a common objective allows a clear determination of the roles of individual nations and allows for guidelines for the contributions of each country. Detailed cooperation is imperative in these areas.

These issues often extend into areas beyond direct economic policy but have significant effects on economic performance. To sum up, the administration is not reluctant or unwilling to engage in international economic cooperation. However, its attitude toward multinational initiatives of this sort is clearly more streamlined and also more selective than that of past administrations.

III

Supply-Side Economics and the Reagan Program

3

RICHARD W. RAHN

Supply-Side Economics: The U.S. Experience

The election of Ronald Reagan was widely viewed as the triumph of the "supply-siders" over the "Keynesians"—yet by midterm the American press had already composed the obituary of "supply-side economics." For many of us who were enthusiastic supporters of the Reagan economic program and who had some impact on its design, the events of recent months are a struggle against those who insist on burying a program that has not been given a fair chance to succeed.

The sections entitled "'Supply-Side Economics': Some Fundamentals" and "The Case for Tax Cuts" were partially adapted from a paper prepared by the author for "The Conference on Constraining Federal Taxing and Spending" at the Hoover Institution, Stanford University, 21–23 October 1981.

Why has this occurred? A number of reasons can be advanced, all of which revolve around a basic misunderstanding of supply-side economics. It frequently has been portrayed as a radical departure from American tradition and thus as a dangerous experiment, while in fact it is nothing more than an update of Adam Smith's principles of the economics of incentives. Our Founding Fathers were extremely aware of the dangers, both to liberty and to economic growth, of large government, excessive government regulation, and high rates of taxation. And indeed, by avoiding such dangers, America grew rapidly from the mid-1700s until the 1930s, largely because it had an unfettered free market with a low level of government participation in the economy and, for the most part, low marginal rates of taxation.

The dominant American economic philosophy—popularly referred to as Keynesian—that began in the early 1930s and lasted until late 1980 will most likely be judged by future historians as an aberration in the history of American economic thought. As practiced in the United States by self-designated Keynesian politicians and some of their economic advisors, Keynesian economics became a system that either ignored or tried to explain away, through "partial equilibrium" reasoning, the disincentive effects of high rates of taxation and regulation on productive economic activity.

Adam Smith and his philosophical forerunners, as well as the American Founding Fathers, had a keen understanding of the importance of incentives for productive economic activity. Thus it is particularly ironic that just as psychologists were becoming more systematic in their analysis and description of the role of incentives (i.e., reinforcers) in human behavior (with the rise of the behavioral school of psychology in the 1930s), American and British economists and politicians were developing a number of public policy prescriptions that contradicted the findings of the behaviorists.

The failure of these policymakers to recognize or ac-

knowledge the disincentives inherent in their policy prescriptions resulted in a slowdown in the rate of real economic
growth in the United States. This, in turn, led to a receptivity
on the part of both voters and their elected representatives
to alternative policy approaches that resulted in the adoption
last August of a supply-side tax program known as the Economic Recovery Tax Act of 1981.

Unfortunately, Congress delayed and tampered with the
tax cut program. Because the tax cuts were postponed, there
was no offsetting fiscal relief to the tighter, yet highly erratic, monetary growth that occurred during 1980 and 1981,
which generated record-high real rates of interest. The
result has been the severe recession, which has been blamed
on a supply-side program that is just beginning.

Only a month after the passage of the Economic Recovery
Tax Act, the Reagan administration called for some tax increases. The U.S. Senate Finance Committee, as a result,
passed a major tax increase on 2 July that will offset many of
the positive effects expected from last year's tax cut. However, unless the supply-side program is eventually put into
place, it is unlikely that the United States will again be able
to achieve a sustained rate of even moderate real economic
growth—and it is apparent from the events of this year that
the necessary changes will not come as quickly and easily as
many had hoped after the 1981 legislative victory.

"Supply-Side Economics": Some Fundamentals

According to Norman B. Ture, a basic characteristic of
supply-side analysis is that

it identifies the initial effects of tax or other fiscal actions in terms
of the changes in relative prices these actions entail and seeks to
describe and measure how households and businesses respond to
these relative price changes. The responses are likely to take the
form of changes in the total amount supplied of one or another production input, hence changes in total output and income. These
second-level income effects are also likely to be powerful influences

on the level and composition of economic activity. The "supply-side" analysis doesn't exclude income as a determinant of economic behavior, but it does hold that the initial effects of fiscal actions cannot be identified as changes in income. In summary terms, the "supply-side" analysis: (1) ascribes to fiscal actions a first-level effect on (explicit or implicit) relative prices, (2) rejects the view that fiscal actions can have a first-level effect on total income, and (3) holds that changes in income result from the responses by households and businesses to the relative price changes generated by fiscal actions.[1]

The U.S. tax system imposes serious impediments to productive economic activity, referred to as the "tax wedge" by supply-side economists. The tax wedge on labor, for example, is the difference between what an employer pays for a worker's services and what the worker actually receives. It involves those taxes an employer has to pay on a worker's wage—such as an employer's share of Social Security, unemployment taxes, etc. In addition, the employee suffers a direct share of the wedge involving such payouts as his share of the Social Security tax and individual income taxes. Since taxes on an employer increase his real labor cost, while the taxes on an employee reduce the employee's real wage, it follows that an increase in taxes on employment lessens both the demand for and the supply of labor. This, in turn, reduces the nation's level of economic output and real per capita income.

The U.S. tax wedge on capital has been even more severe; for example, federal taxes on interest income were as high as 70 percent until this year. Taxes on corporate dividends are even higher when one properly considers the corporate income tax, plus state and local taxes on that income, plus the individual federal income tax on those dividends. The effective tax rate on corporate dividends until 1981 approached 90 percent for some individuals in some states.

The tax on capital gains has been even worse, given the high rates of inflation we have suffered, because there is no inflation adjustment for the cost basis under our system of capital gains taxation. From 1969 through 1978, many people were actually paying heavy capital gains taxes on real capital losses. The tax wedge on capital can also involve indirect taxes on capital, such as the underdepreciation of business plant and equipment that occurred extensively during the past decade.

The tax wedge on capital has led to far less investment than would have otherwise occurred without such high levels of taxation. In turn, this has resulted in far lower productivity growth, far lower real economic growth, and lower per capita incomes.

It has been known since antiquity that tax rates are not the same as tax revenues, and in fact may be inversely correlated in some cases. Adam Smith referred to the counterproductive aspects of taxation a number of times in *The Wealth of Nations,* and at one point stated:

> Every tax ought to be so contrived as both to take out and to keep out of the pockets of the people as little as possible, over and above what it brings into the public treasury of the state. A tax may either take out or keep out of the pockets of the people a great deal more than it brings into the public treasury, in the ... following ways. ... It may obstruct the industry of the people, and discourage them from applying to certain branches of business which might give maintenance and employment to great multitudes. While it obliges the people to pay, it may thus diminish, or perhaps destroy, some of the funds which might enable them more easily to do so.[2]

The understanding that rates affect the supply of factors of production and hence the tax base, which in turn influences the resulting tax revenue, is now commonly referred to as the "Laffer Curve," because of its popularization by Dr. Arthur B. Laffer. Its rather simple notion that tax revenue is equal to the product of the tax base times the tax rate, and hence changes in tax revenues may be either positively or negatively related to changes in tax rates, has often escaped the attention of economic policymakers.

Properly viewed, taxes represent an additional cost of doing business. A tax on labor increases the cost of labor, and a tax on capital increases the cost of capital. These costs become part of the price of the good or activity. Thus, a tax on only one good makes the price of other goods relatively more attractive. A tax on labor, therefore, makes leisure relatively more attractive. A tax on saving makes consumption relatively more attractive. If society desires to increase its rate of economic growth, it needs to make the factor inputs of labor and capital relatively more attractive than the alternative of leisure and consumption.

Is it possible, given today's tax system, to design a tax cut that does not reduce revenues? As Paul Craig Roberts noted in discussing the tax cut debate in 1980:

> From an economic standpoint, it is easy to have an incentive tax cut that doesn't add to the deficit and inflationary pressures. You simply design it not to lose any revenues in the first place. All you have to do is to lower the marginal tax rates on personal income and simultaneously reduce the personal exemption or some of the deductions and credits. That way, the average tax rate, or the amount of taxes people pay on existing earnings, doesn't change. The government doesn't lose any revenues, yet everyone still has an incentive to increase his work effort and savings as a result of getting to keep a larger percentage of his income.[3]

Thus, it is possible to increase the incentives to work, save, and invest, *and* bring about significant increases in economic growth and per capita incomes, without adding to the size of the deficit. Unfortunately, this fact has escaped many public and some private sector policymakers and opinion leaders, as will be shown later in this paper.

Human Behavior and Supply-Side Economics

One of the great ironies of the policies advocated by the political Keynesians is their disregard for the increasing knowledge psychologists have obtained about human behavior. Since the work of J. B. Watson, who is often regarded as the father of the school of behavioral psychology, psychologists have made enormous strides in determining the incentives or reinforcers to many forms of behavior, including productive economic behavior. For instance, B. F. Skinner's use of operant conditioning to identify behavior traceable to reinforcing contingencies is now widely accepted. The basic principle — that behavior is shaped and perhaps even determined by its consequences — is commonly understood. Acts having pleasant consequences tend to be repeated (positive reinforcement), whereas those having unpleasant consequences are likely to be avoided (negative reinforcement). And there are primary and secondary reinforcers. Primary reinforcers such as food, shelter, and clothing satisfy physiological needs, while secondary reinforcers such as money are exchangeable for primary reinforcers that meet either physiological or psychological needs.

Money is the one reinforcer that enables people to acquire most other things that provide positive reinforcement. When a worker makes a decision to take a job, he has analyzed and compared the positive and negative reinforcers and has found the positive reinforcer (in pay) stronger than the negative reinforcers. In the economist's jargon, he obtains net positive utility.

It is clear that a high level of taxation weakens the reinforcer effects of money, and at some point will clearly extinguish the productive behavior. Anyone who understands the law of supply and demand in effect understands operant conditioning. It is always a marvel to see economists who are proficient in price theory disregard the relative price effects of changes in taxation or regulation. Once you acknowledge that taxes and regulations have a price effect, then you need to have some understanding of the elasticity of demand for taxed goods or services in order to get adequate revenue projections.

In this year's tax debate before Congress, proponents of several excise taxes have invariably assumed that the demand for the good to be taxed is perfectly inelastic. Even though every freshman economics student knows that an excise tax on a good will reduce the quantity demanded, the congressional committees and the U.S. Treasury routinely ignore such basic principles in their projections. Tax increases, as a result, rarely provide the revenue projected, and the rate of economic growth afterward is normally overestimated.

The supply-side movement is, in part, a reaction to the simplistic and irrational policies of the political Keynesians. In essence, the modern supply-siders are saying that the success of any economic policy will depend on both the positive and negative reinforcers that determine whether the necessary factors of production will be provided.

The Case for Tax Cuts

The "Kennedy tax cuts" of 1964 and 1965 are often cited as prime examples of supply-side tax cuts, in both their form and their effects. Over a two-year period, individual taxes were reduced by an average of 20 percent. The new range was from 14 to 70 percent instead of the previous 20 to 91 percent.

An extensive review of the Kennedy tax cuts has been made by Bruce Bartlett, deputy staff director of the Joint Economic Committee. He states:

> What did the tax cut actually do for the economy? Virtually all of the econometric studies of the Kennedy tax cut agree that it was highly stimulative to the economy. Arthur Okun, chairman of the Council of Economic Advisers under President Johnson, has stated that the tax cuts of 1964 are credited with a $25 billion contribution to our GNP by mid-1965, a $20 billion effect by the end of 1965, and an ultimate $36 billion increment. Similar estimates have been made by Lawrence Klein, Data Resources, Inc.; Wharton Econometric Forecasting Associates, Inc.; and the Congressional Budget Office.[4]

Walter Heller, in 1977 testimony before the Joint Economic Committee, stated:

What happened to the tax cut in 1965 is difficult to pin down, but insofar as we are able to isolate it, it did seem to have a tremendously stimulative effect, a multiplied effect on the economy. It was a major factor that led to our running a $3 billion surplus by the middle of 1965 before escalation in Vietnam struck us. It was a $12 billion tax cut which would be about $33 or $34 billion in today's terms, and within one year the revenues into the Federal Treasury were already above what they had been before the tax cut. . . . Did it pay for itself in increased revenues? I think the evidence is very strong that it did.[5]

The most recent U.S. example of a supply-side tax cut, where there is evidence of its effects, was the reduction of the capital gains tax in the 1978 tax bill. The tax reduction was accomplished by increasing the capital gains exclusion to 60 percent from the previous 50 percent and reducing the maximum capital gains tax from 49.125 percent to 28 percent.

In their 1979 analysis of the capital gains tax change, Richard W. Rahn and Mari Lee Dunn summarized their findings as follows:

(1) Those portions of the capital gains that are taxes on capital rather than on the return to capital are clearly destructive. Since the revenue such taxation provides the government, in the short run erodes the capital stock while greatly discouraging capital investment, the result is lower productivity and slower economic growth. (2) Most of the capital gains that have been realized in the United States in this decade have not been real gains, but merely apparent gains resulting from inflation. The taxation of these gains has in effect been a tax on capital.

(3) A reduction in capital gains tax rates will affect tax revenues in three ways. First, a reduction in the statutory rate will cause an increase in the amount of realized capital gains. Second, the rate reduction will stimulate additional investment activity, which will in turn lead to economic growth, more job creation, and therefore, greater tax revenues from ordinary income. Third, the incentive for reducing the lock-in of invested capital will lead to additional turnovers of stock and other capital assets after the effective date of the capital gains rate reduction, and thus will increase tax revenues. (4) The preponderance of the evidence from the recent studies of capital gains taxation in the U.S. indicated that the stimulation of investment activity as well as the reduction of the lock-in effect

from the 1978 capital gains tax reduction will, in all likelihood, not reduce government tax revenues in the short run and will increase tax revenues in the long run. (5) There would be substantial benefits to the economy over the long run, including increased employment, greater productivity, and increased tax revenue if illusory capital gains stemming from inflation were not taxed.[6]

These conclusions have been verified by further evidence of the beneficial aspects of the capital gains tax reduction that have been accumulating since the date of enactment of the reduction. Specifically, new public stock offerings and new venture capital by 1980 increased fivefold over the 1978 level. In addition, the American Council for Capital Formation reports:

> Taxes paid on capital gains income increased from $8.3 billion in 1978 under the old tax rates, to $10.1 billion in 1979, the first year of the new lower tax rates—a gain of $1.8 billion. The largest increase in realized capital gains came from "fat cats," taxpayers with adjusted gross incomes in excess of $100,000. Their share of reported capital gains increased from about 29 percent in 1978 to nearly 41 percent in 1979, according to the latest Treasury figures.[7]

The multiple taxation of corporate income, as was indicated earlier, long has been recognized as the major drag on capital income and as a severe disincentive to investment—noncorporate as well as corporate.[8] Even ignoring the state taxes, an individual in the 70 percent bracket received only 15.6 cents in after-tax income from a dollar of precorporate tax earnings paid out as dividends.

Many economic models now indicate that favorable effects would result from less discriminatory tax treatment of capital. Supply-siders such as Norman Ture, Arthur Laffer, and Michael Evans have produced such results, as have the models of Otto Eckstein and Lawrence Klein.[9] For instance, Eckstein testified to the Joint Economic Committee last year that "the supply effects of [Kemp-Roth-type] personal tax reductions are important, and are little affected by the government spending cuts."[10] The New York Stock Exchange study conducted by Wharton Econometric Forecasting Associates, Inc., found that much stronger real growth and lower inflation would result if "tax policies were implemented in the expectation of raising the investment/GNP ratio."[11]

Reductions in tax rates on income from capital would benefit labor as well. As Ture pointed out in a 1973 study that examined both the empirical and the theoretical case against differential taxation of capital and labor:

> The present tax structure in the United States is heavily biased against private saving and investment. . . . Constructive tax reform would seek a more nearly neutral tax system, and . . . saving and capital accumulation would accelerate under a tax structure which adhered more closely to the neutrality criterion. The higher rate of saving and investment in turn would increase the rate of growth of total output and would enhance the advance in labor's productivity and real earnings.[12]

Finally, there is considerable evidence that reductions in marginal tax rates on labor income induce an increase in labor supply, at least among certain segments of the labor force. Joines cites spouses of workers, small business proprietors, upper-income taxpayers, and individuals on Social Security who lose benefits when they earn more than a minimum amount.[13]

Although the United States has one of the lowest overall tax rates among developed countries, it ranks high in two taxes critical to investment and growth: corporate income taxes and property taxes (including net wealth, estates, and gifts). Thus, the U.S. tax burden on productive capital is relatively high, which helps to explain our low growth rates.

Emphasis on the deficit rather than on the way it is financed can be counterproductive. If a country has a high savings rate, a given deficit will produce less in the way of inflationary or crowding-out pressures than in a country with a low deficit and a low savings rate. Virtually all of the great economic success stories of the past thirty years have been in countries such as Japan, West Germany, and Hong Kong, which have had very low or declining personal and corporate income tax rates during their periods of most rapid growth.

The Reagan Economic Program: Promise, Reality, and Outlook

President Reagan ran for office on essentially a supply-side economic platform. There were four major components to his economic program. The first was to reduce and stabilize the rate of monetary growth in order to bring inflation and interest rates down. A second component was to reduce government regulation by eliminating regulations that were not justified on a reasonable cost-benefit basis. The third component was to reduce the growth rate of government spending and to bring it down as a percentage of GNP from approximately 23 percent when President Reagan took office to 19.5 percent. Finally, the program advocated reducing the tax impediments on work, saving, and investment. Specifically, the major first-order tax changes were to enact the Kemp-Roth proposal to reduce rates in each tax bracket by 10 percent in 1981, 1982, and 1983, for a total of 30 percent. Tax rates thereafter would be indexed to offset inflation. Congress, in addition, was to enact the Accelerated Cost Recovery Act proposal, also known as 10-5-3.

Eighteen months later, it is clear that the Reagan economic program has fallen far short of its promises in a number of areas. First, the monetary policy goals have not been met. Monetary policy is conducted by the Federal Reserve, an independent government agency. The Fed has brought down the average rate of monetary growth, but it has done it in a highly erratic manner. M1 growth was very rapid in early 1981, negligible for eight months thereafter, and then relatively rapid in late 1981 and early 1982. The result of these policies has been to bring down the rate of inflation from over 12 percent in 1980 to approximately only 3.5 percent in the first six months of 1982. Yet at the same time, nominal interest rates have remained high, resulting in record-high real rates of interest. These record rates of real interest were largely responsible for the recession and have delayed the recovery.

The administration's efforts to reduce regulatory impediments have met with much greater, though not total, success. An effective mechanism has been set up in the Office of Management and Budget to review new regulations for the purpose of insuring that they are justified on a reasonable cost-benefit basis, and that they are undertaken in the least expensive manner. The result has been to reduce greatly the number of new regulations emanating from the federal government. Very little progress, however, has been made in repealing much of the existing body of regulation.

The original Reagan administration goal of bringing government spending down to 19.5 percent of the GNP thus far has also failed. Despite the headlines in many newspapers, government spending has not been reduced, and the so-called "entitlement" or "people" programs are continuing to grow faster than either the rate of private sector growth or the rate of inflation. Although some progress has been made in reducing the growth of nondefense or transfer payment spending, the overall result has been disappointing. Fiscal year 1982 will culminate in a record-high level of government spending as a percentage of GNP, 23.5 percent.

In August of 1981, Congress passed, and the president signed into law, the Economic Recovery Tax Act of 1981. The act embodied many of the president's tax policy proposals and contained a number of other provisions that in the long run will be beneficial. Unfortunately, the cornerstone of the president's program, the reduction in personal rates, was both diluted and delayed. The first personal rate reduction of 5 percent did not occur until October 1981, and the first 10 percent rate reduction occurred as recently as 1 July 1982. Because of previously legislated Social Security tax increases and tax bracket creep, most Americans had real increases in tax rates during both 1981 and the first six months of 1982. This increasing tax burden, coupled with a stringent and erratic monetary policy, not only drove the economy into recession but also greatly increased the size of current budget deficits and of those projected for future years. High interest rates and big deficits combined to produce a climate of fear among many members of Congress and the American public, leading to calls for a number of irrational and clearly counterproductive proposals such as major increases in taxes and various forms of credit controls and spending programs to combat unemployment.

Members of the administration still do not fully understand the supply-side program and the difference between tax rates and tax revenues. Unfortunately, they were able to convince the president to veer away from his original economic program. These events illustrate a major problem with Western democracies: the political cycle is shorter than the economic cycle, and even well-intentioned governments have a hard time maintaining the steady and steadfast course that is often necessary to bring fundamental corrections to their economies.

The tax increase bill approved by the Senate Finance Committee on 2 July 1982, and supported by the administration, reduced the business portion of the 1981 tax cut by about 66 percent. Most of these proposed tax increases would have come from saving. Overall, the 1981 tax cut bill was reduced by about 23 percent by the Finance Committee proposal. To date, there clearly has not been a total refutation of the supply-side program, but there is a concerted effort under way to diminish its thrust. The great danger is that unless a good many of the tax cuts are allowed to remain in place, and unless Congress does come to grips with the problem of entitlements spending, the economy will not be able to sustain a reasonable rate of economic growth. The political battle will then begin again between the strong supply-side advocates who will claim the program was never given a chance, and opponents who claim the program did not succeed because it was conceptually flawed. Despite the short-run reverses, I am optimistic over the long run, basically because of the growing economic sophistication of the American people. Despite our continuing economic difficulties, the American people continue to communicate through public opinion polls and by electoral decisions that they want a reduction both in the rate of growth in government spending and in taxation.

Those of us who have been arguing for the supply-side program for a number of years were to some extent surprised by how quick and easy our victories in 1980 and 1981 seemed to have come. Our difficulties this year have brought us back to the reality that the battle for good economic policy will require a long-term commitment to hard work and tenacity in educating the American people and news media to the fundamental fact that long-run economic growth can be obtained only with a system that provides strong incentives for working, saving, and investing.

4

J. HAROLD McCLURE

THOMAS D. WILLETT

Understanding the Supply-Siders

Debate over the Reagan economic program has been greatly complicated by widespread public confusion about just what is meant by the term "supply-side economics." At the center of this confusion is a failure, among both ordinary citizens and professional commentators, to appreciate the distinction between what amount to two major variants of supply-side thinking—a moderate or "mainstream" supply-side view,

We are indebted to the Lincoln Foundation for financial support for the research underlying this paper, and to King Banaian, David Berson, Marian Brown, Gary Evans, Susan Feigenbaum, Richard Sweeney, and Frank Wykoff for helpful comments on an earlier draft.

and a "radical" version of the doctrine. Mainstream supply-siders include such figures as Michael Boskin and Martin Feldstein, while prominent proponents of the radical school include George Gilder, Arthur Laffer, Robert Mundell, Richard Rahn, and Jude Wanniski.[1] Not all prominent supply-siders fit neatly into these two categories, but the distinction is nonetheless broadly accurate, and public discussion has tended to blur the division in a way that makes the Reagan strategy difficult to evaluate.

Radical and mainstream supply-siders agree on one essential point: government taxing and spending policies have important effects on incentives to work, save, and invest. What divides the two schools is the question of degree. Mainstreamers acknowledge that supply will respond positively to reductions in tax rates, but they doubt that the responses will be robust enough to support two key tenets of the radical version: that tax cuts will pay for themselves and that they will be anti-inflationary.

Mainstream supply-siders are also skeptical of the radicals' contention that tax cuts and changes in the money supply can occur without substantially affecting aggregate demand. Thus the mainstream school questions radical supply-side explanations for the upsurge in growth following the Kennedy administration's tax cuts in 1964 and 1965. In the mainstream view, whenever such tax cuts have managed to pay for themselves, demand rather than supply effects have dominated. Thus, while for mainstreamers it is empirically plausible that in times of recession tax cuts might stimulate sufficient increased economic activity to boost government revenues, the revenue gains would result from an increase in demand relative to supply. Of course, such increases aggravate inflationary pressures.

What the mainstreamers emphasize is that the basic case for tax and spending cuts and reductions in monetary growth does not depend on the radical supply-side assumption that tax cuts *by themselves* will raise government revenues and reduce inflation.[2] Mainstream supply-siders recognize the incentive effects of taxation, but tend to see them operating over the longer run. They believe that tax cuts have both benefits and costs, and they locate the rationale for the Reagan program in its effect on the long-term health of the economy rather than in its ability—or failure—to produce a short-term "supply-side miracle."[3]

It is the emphasis on incentives that constitutes the key contribution of supply-side thinking, whether mainstream or radical, to economics as a whole. The Keynesian tradition has tended to stress the effects of taxes and government spending policies on aggregate demand, paying little or no attention to the impact such policies have on incentives. In dwelling on this Keynesian omission, radical supply-siders have not been totally unfair. At the same time, it would be an exaggeration to claim—as radical supply-siders come close to doing—that mainstream Keynesians have simply ignored the supply side of the economy. The Keynesian economists on the Council of Economic Advisers during the Kennedy and Johnson administrations paid considerable attention to investment incentives and their probable effects on long-run growth. Indeed, the leading contributors to growth theory may be described as Keynesians.

In short, among economists generally, there is wide agreement that the effects of government policy on investment are crucial, and that a combination of loose fiscal and tight monetary policies works against investment. In the end, whether in formulating policy more attention should be paid to aggregate demand or to supply effects is a technical economic issue and depends upon a) the importance of short-run as opposed to long-run effects, b) the degree to which demand can affect output, and c) the relative magnitude of supply effects as compared with the impact of short-run demand.

In recent years the economics profession as a whole has seen heightened interest in supply-side effects, and numerous contributors to mainstream economic literature have attempted to delineate the factors that determine potential or "full-employment" output and the causes of slowdown in productivity growth. There have been a number of attempts to develop improved estimates of the quantitative effects of government tax and subsidy policies on savings, investment, labor supply, and unemployment. Both politically liberal and conservative economists have made such contributions.[4] This literature has led to the recognition that the changing composition of the labor force has increased the noninflationary level of unemployment; that the oil shocks have reduced the economic usefulness of a portion of the capital stock, which may lower the full-employment level of the capacity utilization rate; and that changes in unemployment compensation may encourage the practice of temporary layoffs. There remains a great deal of professional controversy concerning the magnitudes of these effects, but the evidence indicates that they are not trivial for policy purposes.

The Impact of Incentives

On the level of theory, neoclassical economics suggests that tax cuts have both substitution and income effects on labor and saving decisions. Under the substitution effect, tax cuts should be expected to encourage more labor and less leisure, as well as less consumption today in favor of saving for future consumption. But the income effect works in the opposite direction in both cases, encouraging less labor and more consumption.[5] Therefore, a priori reasoning not only fails to support large labor and savings responses, but it cannot alone even support a positive response. The initial empirical studies typically found zero or very small effects from tax cuts, and consequently many economists have argued that the elasticity of labor supply and savings is practically zero.[6] More recent work by Michael Boskin, Martin Feldstein, and others have found substantial positive elasticities, but the latest studies suggest that Boskin's and Feldstein's results overestimated the responses, so the exact magnitude of these elasticities is professionally controversial.[7] On the whole, the findings suggest that tax cuts may increase labor supply and that higher after-tax real interest rates may possibly raise savings. While these effects may be large enough to have significance for policymaking, they are not large enough to support the radical supply-side case.

To argue that incentives matter, however, is not to argue that tax cuts pay for themselves. The radical supply-side school originally claimed that the Kemp-Roth income tax cuts would so increase potential output that tax revenues, which are the product of tax rates and output, would actually rise. They also argued that since savings would rise, consumption demand would fall. If consumption fell, inflation would be reduced and investment increased.[8]

But radical supply-siders have tended to leap illogically from arguments for positive effects to arguments for large effects. Radical supply-siders offer two mutually exclusive claims that do not exhaust the universe of possibilities. For example, let's write two propositions: (a) tax rate cuts do not increase output and may decrease it, and (b) tax rate cuts greatly increase output and will therefore raise tax revenues. The refutation of (a) does not imply (b). Proposition (a) requires a zero or negative elasticity of output with respect to tax rates. Proposition (b) requires that this elasticity exceed unity so that the output effects will dominate the rate reduction.[9] A third possibility exists: a tax rate reduction may raise output with an elasticity less than unity, so revenues still fall. Whether this elasticity exceeds unity or not determines which side of the Laffer Curve the economy is on.

A similar difficulty appears in the controversy over tax rates, savings, and consumption. For consumption demand to decline relative to total output requires more than a rise in the savings ratio. Total savings (the sum of private savings and taxes) determines what happens to consumption, and small increases in the savings ratio will not offset large tax rate reductions. Tax cuts that do not have large savings effects will increase private consumption.[10]

The Impact of Demand

Likewise, the radical supply-side school has tended to leap from the defensible position that aggregate demand effects are often overemphasized to the proposition that the demand effects do not matter—a view shared by proponents of the extreme "rational expectations" or "new classical" school who imagine that demand shifts will be fully anticipated.[11] Supply-side proponents often imply that any historical movement in output is owing to movements in potential output. In this sense, they accept the classical Say's Law, which asserts that aggregate demand always adjusts to aggregate supply. If such were the case, the rises in output following the 1922, 1924, and 1964 tax cuts would be evidence for the supply-side hypothesis. By contrast, monetarists and Keynesians emphasize that actual output can fall *below* potential output in the short run, if demand is insufficient to fully employ productive resources. In traditional macroeconomics, as long as actual output remains below potential output, the movement of the economy is dictated by demand factors, and supply factors have no effect on real GNP (although unemployment and inflation will depend upon supply events to the degree that they depend upon the difference between demand and supply).[12] In fact, one clue as to whether an output increase is from increased labor supply and/or productivity on the one hand, or from demand using preexisting excess supply on the other, is the behavior of the unemployment rate. Unemployment fell from 6.7 to 2.4 percent in 1923, from 5.0 to 3.2 percent in 1925, and from 5.7 to 3.8 percent during the Kennedy tax cut era. In all three instances, therefore, it seems that demand, and not supply, was the crucial factor.

In the Keynesian model, tax cuts raise consumption demand, causing multiplier effects on output. Therefore, tax rate reductions do raise actual output, if it is below potential output. If the Keynesian multiplier is sufficiently large, then government revenues may also rise.[13] For example, the Dornbusch and Fischer account of the Kennedy tax cuts calculates that the tax cut of $13 billion led to increased demand of $36 billion, just the amount of the estimated excess supply in 1964.[14] With marginal tax rates near 50 percent, the induced $18 billion Keynes-Laffer demand effect on tax revenues dominated the initial effect, but this calculation is purely a demand—not a supply—explanation, and requires that excess supply previously existed. While a portion of the revenue gains from the tax cuts may indeed have been supply induced, the radical supporters rarely even mention the demand side, and it seems extremely doubtful that such supply-side effects were anywhere close to the demand effects in quantitative significance.

The Inflation Issue

Radical supply-siders criticize both monetarists and Keynesians for their emphasis on the need to reduce aggregate demand in order to slow inflation. The supply-side solution, of course, is to increase supply instead. The difficulty from the standpoint of conventional analysis is how the latter can be accomplished without expanding demand even more, leading to increasing rather than decreasing inflation. One of the most startling of the radical supply-side claims is that tax cuts are by themselves anti-inflationary. Of course, such a result can follow directly from assuming away demand effects while assuming supply increases. In more general terms, the radical argument would be that the expansionary effects on aggregate demand are less than the expansionary effects on aggregate supply. Yet while monetarists and Keynesians would differ in their views of the size of the

short-run demand effects that would result from a cut in
taxes unaccompanied by monetary expansion, there is no
broadly based empirical support for the view that supply
effects would be greater than demand effects in the short
run. As a *long-run* proposition in a monetarist world, the
view that tax cuts are anti-inflationary may be true. But as a
short-term description this is empirically implausible. Certainly, it is nearly impossible to generate by tax cuts the type
of short-run acceleration of economic growth combined with
a deceleration of inflation that was forecast in the initial
Reagan administration economic projections.

The Investment Issue

One can raise similar objections to the proposition that an income tax cut will stimulate investment by so increasing output and savings that the increased consumption does not
crowd out private investment. This can easily occur with expansion of aggregate demand when there is a good deal of
slack in the economy, but would require implausibly high
elasticities of supply and savings responsiveness if the economy were already at full employment.

It should be noted here that radical supply-siders often
argue that savings responses will be tremendously high,
based on the experiences with responses to temporary tax
surcharges or rebates (see, for example, the preceding
chapter by Rahn). The evidence is consistent with the hypothesis that these temporary tax changes have been almost
fully offset by compensating shifts in savings, leaving aggregate demand little changed. But this is easily explained in
traditional terms by the permanent income or life-cycle
models, which argue that rational individuals will keep their
consumption levels roughly unchanged in the face of transitory fluctuations in income. Since temporary tax surcharges and rebates are classic examples of fluctuations in
income that are considered transitory, we would expect con-

sumption spending to be little affected, implying that there would be close to a one-for-one offsetting change in savings in the short run. Since the supply-siders appropriately stress that the beneficial incentive effects from income tax cuts will fully occur only if the tax cuts are expected to be "permanent," it is quite illegitimate to infer information about savings responses to "permanent" tax cuts such as the Reagan program from responses to temporary tax changes such as the 1968 surcharge. Economic analysis clearly indicates that the savings response to "permanent" changes will be a good deal smaller.

Other Issues

A third example of supply-side leaps in logic in the presentation of evidence is the tendency to argue that the effects of certain types of tax cuts imply similar effects for income tax cuts. Supply-siders have made valuable contributions in highlighting cases where particular types of taxes have been highly distorting and even counterproductive in generating tax revenues. For example, Richard Rahn presents evidence that this was the case with respect to capital gains taxation. An analysis by Minarik argues to the contrary that when other factors are held constant, this tax cut did not fully pay for itself; but nonetheless the elasticity of response was clearly quite high.[15] This example still does not tell us anything about the *degree* of responsiveness to the Kemp-Roth Reagan income tax cuts, however.

A fourth and final example is the concern with budget deficits. Supply-siders argue quite convincingly that one should not be automatically worried about deficits per se. Whether deficits pose problems or not depends crucially on the cause. This is a view common to both monetarists and Keynesians who, for example, distinguish between deficits caused by a recession, which are not a source of concern, and those that do or would occur at full employment, which are.

What is troublesome is that supply-side arguments about why one should not always be concerned about deficits are frequently presented in ways that can easily give the false impression that one should never worry about deficits. Supply-siders are correct to argue that there has been too much simple-minded focus on the size of the current deficit, which is to a substantial extent a result of the recession. The disturbing feature is that under current policies a large deficit is projected to remain in future years even after full employment is restored.

Conclusions

What has the experience under President Reagan's economic policies taught us about the validity of supply-side economics? It would be very easy but very misleading for critics to argue that the declining output is evidence that the supply elasticities are negative. Radical supply-siders make an interesting case when they point out that the timing of the tax cuts adversely affected the operation of the incentives. In addition, some versions of the supply-side case argue that the full responses may take several years; thus evidence from the first year does not tell the whole tale. The theme of rapid supply-side recovery, as put forth by Representative Kemp, may be refuted by current evidence, but not the view that tax cuts would pay for themselves over several years.[16]

However, even before the Reaganomics experiment, there existed a massive amount of evidence indicating that while incentives matter, the large responses claimed by radical supply-siders were unfounded. We believe that the major lesson to be drawn from Reaganomics is that demand factors, including monetary policy, do matter in the short run. While there was already plenty of evidence on this point before President Reagan was elected, the current recession provides further strong confirmation.

As a final point, we should like to emphasize the

mainstream supply-side argument that the best way to stimulate more rapid rates of economic growth, over the long run, is to revamp the tax structure specifically to increase the incentives for savings and investment rather than to focus primarily on across-the-board income tax cuts. This, we believe, is an important complement to the adoption of overall tax and spending policies that keep the size of the full-employment deficit small so as to limit the amount of private investment that is crowded out.

RESPONSE

Arthur B. Laffer: "Not Enough Incentives"

I want to focus on the incentive approach and the Reagan administration's economic policies. There is crisis virtually everywhere in the world. The crisis is neither unique to the U.S. nor the most severe in the U.S. If you take a look at Poland or Iran or Great Britain, you find that literally everywhere, crisis is at hand. Institutions are under radical attack, and people are trying to find something that works. The U.S., however, is in a unique position in its attempt to reassociate effort and reward.

The political situation is very analagous to what was occurring very early in the 1960s. If you remember, in 1960 President Kennedy's run for office against Richard Nixon had two major campaign themes. One theme was that the Eisenhower administration had let our defenses fall, and we had to increase defense spending and the space program dramatically. The other side of his program was that the economy had been in the doldrums during the Eisenhower administration, and we had to get America going and growing again. Kennedy proposed massive tax cuts. When he came into office in 1961, he met with a lot of problems. For example, in 1961 we had a deficit of $3.9 billion. That was a huge deficit. The *New York Times* attacked Kennedy for trying to increase defense spending and cut taxes. In fact, he was being asked all the time to give up one of the two programs.

He cut taxes a lot in the early 1960s, and it was then that Kennedy gave his speech about myths, in which he talked about problems that are basically the same as those facing Ronald Reagan today. He said that the real problem in America is not lies, because lies are so easily uncovered and shown to be false. He argued that the real impediments to truth and good policymaking are myths, which have a major kernel of truth in them but which are mostly deceptive and misleading to policymakers. The example Jack Kennedy gave of the true myth in America was the idea that you can balance the budget by raising taxes: when Eisenhower came into office in 1953, the first thing he did was to veto Robert Taft's tax cut at the advice of Arthur Burns. And yet in 1958 we had a $12.2 billion deficit—the largest peace-time deficit up to that time—and a slow economy. On the other hand, Harry Truman in 1944 pegged the dollar to gold with the Bretton Woods agreement, and in 1945 cut personal income taxes and corporate taxes dramatically. Subsequently, in the 1945–1949 period, we had enormous real growth. The unemployment rate never went as high as 4 percent; long-term interest rates never went as high as 2 percent; our inflation rate dropped from about 20 percent right on down to zero. We had four out of five years when the budget was in surplus after the Truman policies.

Kennedy argued that deficits are not the cause of bad economics. They are caused by bad economics. You can never handle deficits directly. The two primary features that cause large deficits are interest rates and high unemployment. Inflation reduces the real value of nominal liabilities. If you look at the market's anticipation of this, you can see that interest rates in the marketplace have two components. One is the principle repayment component—an inflation premium—and the other portion we call the debt service component. One of the largest and fastest growing items in the federal budget has been interest payments on the national debt. The national debt is about $800 billion. Every one percent increase in the interest rates on the national debt increases government spending by about $8 billion per year. If we were to lower interest rates by 10 percentage points, we would be able to reduce government spending by about $80 billion annually.

Every time a person is unemployed he has no income and pays no taxes, and the government loses receipts. Likewise, he gets welfare, food stamps, and unemployment compensation. Unemployment increases government spending. The OMB (Office of Management and Budget) estimates that for every one percent increase in the unemployment rate, the deficit swells by $25 billion annually. If we could drop our unemployment rate from 9 percent to 4 percent, we would be able to reduce the federal government deficit by about $125 billion. Those numbers are enough to offset any projected deficits on into the future of the U.S.

The problem is not the budget deficit. The problem is high unemployment, high interest rates, and high inflation. Never in our history have we balanced a budget or had fiscal solvency when we've had high interest rates, high inflation, and high unemployment. Kennedy argued that you can never reduce unemployment by raising tax rates on productive factors of production.

But the U.S. is in just that position. You can see it elsewhere. What country in Western Europe has the lowest marginal tax rate? It is Switzerland. What's the one country in Western Europe with a balanced budget? Switzerland. Does Britain have high enough taxes for you? Does it have a big enough deficit? Margaret Thatcher dramatically raised taxes in Britain. Britain's deficit has increased tremendously. Sweden has very high taxes and a very big deficit. I think Belgium's deficit is 12 percent of GNP. Hong Kong has low taxes and rapid economic growth, and it has fiscal solvency. Compare Bermuda with Jamaica. Jamaica has the highest tax rates in all the islands. Bermuda has no income tax at all. Which one has more poverty, more despair, and more unemployment? Which one is bankrupt? Which one has taxicab drivers who can send their kids to finishing schools in Switzerland? What city in the United States before Koch became its mayor had the highest tax rates and also the biggest deficit? You don't balance budgets by raising taxes. My daughter understands what David Stockman can't comprehend.

Our current problems stem from the violation of another basic principle: you never should delay price cuts or tax cuts. But that is exactly what we've done. How much would you shop at a store a week before they have a discount sale? The IRS never discriminates between income earned in January and income earned in December. A 5 percent tax cut in October is exactly a 1.25 percent cut across the whole year. So in 1981 we had a 1.25 percent cut in tax rates. This year we have a 10 percent cut in tax rates. Next year we're going to have a 20 percent cut in tax rates. And in 1984, it's going to be a 25 percent cut in tax rates. There are enough lawyers and accountants in this country to show you how to delay the realization of income until next year when you will face lower tax rates. The delay will even affect actual production decisions. Taxes affect not only the composition of production and the location of production, but the temporal presence of production. What we've done is delayed those tax cuts and thus delayed their positive effects.

There are many other examples of reverse policies. An obvious one is the Social Security payroll tax. As you know, Social Security benefits are primarily indexed to the Consumer Price Index (CPI) with a very minor lag, yet the payroll taxes are not indexed to the CPI. They are indexed to a wage index of two years ago. Wages of two years ago rose enormously. Last year's wages rose enormously. This year wages are rising almost not at all. But this year, our payroll tax increases are based upon wages of two years ago, which means that we have an enormous real payroll tax increase this year. We're going to have an enormous real payroll tax increase next year. But by 1984, payroll tax increases are going to be very minor. Such distortions affect the allocation of resources.

At the same time, there are enormous disincentives for people to try to help themselves. This is why Reagan proposed an enterprise zones plan to try to create tax savings in the inner cities, and a plan not to cut welfare benefits to those who truly need it. Six years ago, I proposed that for any firm that located in the inner city, the maximum tax on profits of its inner-city plant would be 10 percent. If it were to employ a person who was a principal resident, neither the company nor the resident would pay payroll tax, up to $10,000 a year income. Also, we should get rid of the teenage minimum wage. The only way inner-city teenagers get the requisite skills to earn wages above the minimum is through on-the-job training. But when they go on to the job market, they aren't worth the minimum wage, so they are unemployed a couple of years after being out of school. After being unemployed a couple of years, they become unemployable. The plan we proposed five years ago is that all government spending directed toward the inner cities have a mandated requirement of a thorough review of building codes, regulations, restrictions, and requirements to make sure that they are not anti—economic development.

Other programs are needed. One of them is monetary reform. No one cares about the quantity of money. All we care about is the quality of money. The real function of the state, as long as it is going to have a monopoly on the production of this product, is to guarantee the quality of such product. You don't care how much money there is if it's worthless. The sole function of the state is to guarantee the value of that currency. To guarantee the quality of the money is not to have a quantity rule but to have a price rule. It's basically to go back to a price rule where you can fix interest rates; the best of all price rules is to make the dollar convertible into a bundle of commodities or perhaps a specific commodity. Historically, that commodity in the U.S. has been gold, but it doesn't have to be gold at all. If you knew that the dollar thirty years from now was going to be worth exactly what it is today, what do you think would happen to long-term interest rates? They'd go down sharply.

In sum, my view is that once sizeable tax cuts come into effect, you are going to see an enormous expansion in the U.S. economy in the mid and late 1980s, starting about 1984. It will make the go-go '60s look slow. It will make the roaring '20s look slow, too.

IV

Controlling Spending: The 1981–82 Tax and Spending Program

5

ATTIAT F. OTT

Controlling Government Spending

The Reagan administration budget plan for 1983–84 calls for a reversal of the spending patterns of the past decade. The most visible change is to be in defense spending, where the annual rate of growth between 1981 and 1984 is projected to be about double that between 1973 and 1981. The second significant change is the growth rate of the so-called "uncontrollable" programs, specifically Social Security, Medicare and Medicaid, and off-budget outlays. Finally, perhaps most importantly, there is to be a retrenchment of federal involvement in activities within the so-called "merit goods" category: education, training and manpower, and social services. (See tables 1 and 2 for an overview as well as a detailed summary of program changes outlined in the Reagan budget.)

Table 1
The Reagan Administration Budget Outlays by Function, FY 1981–1984
(in billions of dollars)

	1981	1982	1983	1984	Average annual growth rates 1972/81	Average annual growth rates 1981/84
Budget outlays						
National defense and international affairs	170.8	198.6	233.1	265.3	.08	.15
Social Security	137.9	154.6	173.5	188.5	.14	.10
Interest	95.4	99.1	112.5	116.2	.16	.07
Other benefits for individuals:						
Education	15.0	15.4	13.1	10.3	.14	-.12
Training and manpower	9.7	6.0	3.4	4.0	.13	-.30
Social services	6.1	6.4	5.1	5.0	.06	-.07
Health	65.9	73.4	78.1	84.9	.15	.08
Income security other than Social Security	102.2	96.3	88.2	86.3	.16	-.06
Other fiscal operations	54.0	75.5	50.6	45.4	.04	-.06
Off-budget outlays	21.0	19.7	15.7	14.3	.18[a]	-.13

[a]Off-budget outlays were nil in 1972; the growth rate was calculated for the period 1975–1981.

Source: *The Budget of the United States Government, FY 1983.*

Table 2
Summary of Spending Targets
(in billions of dollars)

Programs targeted for reduction

	1982	1983	1984
1. Direct expenditures	(−13.1)	(−56.6)	(−76.9)
Entitlement programs:	−12.0	−27.6	−32.3
Enacted	(−10.6)	(−14.8)	(−14.2)
Proposed	(−1.4)	(−12.8)	(−18.1)
Management initiative	−1.1	−14.8	−18.5
Discretionary and other programs	—	−14.2	−26.1
2. Credit expenditures[a]	(−3.2)	(−2.6)	(−.6)
REA:			
D. Loans	—	−.4	0
G. Loan commitments	−.9	−.5	0
FmHA:			
D. Loans	−.1	−.05	−.01
G. Loan commitments	(+5.0)	(+6.4)	N.F.
GNMA:			
G. Loan commitments	(+5.0)	(+6.9)	N.F.
EX-IM banks:			
D. Loans	−1.0	−.6	−.6
G. Loan commitments	−.6	−.6	0
SBA			
D. Loans	−.1	−.2	N.F.
G. Loan commitments	−.5	−.3	0

Program increases: Discretionary and autonomous

	1982	1983	1984
1. Direct expenditures	(68.2)	(71.5)	(56.7)
National defense	27.7	33.6	31.9
Social Security	16.0	18.9	15.0
Health	7.5	4.7	6.8
Net interest	14.3	13.6	1.7
Research and development:			
NASA	—	.1	—
NSF	.1	—	.1
NEP	—	—	.3
Medicare coverage of federal employees[a]	—	.6	.9
2. Credit expenditures[a]	(10.5)	(13.8)	(.5)
FmHA:			
G. Loan commitments	5.0	6.4	—
GNMA:			
G. Loan commitments	5.0	6.9	—
MBA[b]	.5	.5	.5
3. Revenue enhancement and user charge	(.4)	(16.9)	(24.3)
Railroad retirement	.2	1.7	1.8
Management efficiency	.2	5.5	5.5
User fees	.2	2.5	3.5
Tax revisions:			
Completed contract accounts	—	3.3	5.0
Corporate minimum tax	—	2.3	4.6
Other	—	1.6	3.9

[a] D = Direct; G = Guaranteed; N.F. = Not Funded.

[b] Minority Business Assistance.

Source: *The Budget of the United States Government, FY 1983; Major Themes and Additional Budget Details, FY 1983.*

It is worth noting that significant budget reductions will not be felt until 1984; budget increases will still be larger than reductions for fiscal years 1982 and 1983. Only in 1984, when budget cuts for direct expenditures will be 35 percent higher than increases, does the plan call for the overall budget spending to be effectively reduced.

The degree of reversal in priorities becomes especially clear when one compares the projected Reagan budget with that projected by President Carter (see tables 3 and 4). From the data, a few observations may be made:

- In the Reagan budget there is a dramatic reduction in the spending category labeled "benefit payments for individuals." The average annual rate of growth is projected to decline from 11.1 percent in 1981−82 to 5.3 percent in 1983−84. This is in contrast with the Carter administration budget plan, which had projected an average annual growth rate of 10.7 percent for 1981−82 and 9.6 percent in 1983−84.

- The Reagan plan calls for a slowdown in the rate of growth of total outlays from an average annual rate of 11 percent experienced in 1981−82, to a rate of 6.4 percent in 1983−84. The Carter administration projected an annual growth rate for total outlays of 8.9 percent for 1983−84.

- Although slated for more, the Reagan budget provides for a similar *absolute* increase in defense spending, from an annual growth rate of 17.3 percent for fiscal year 1981−82 to 14.4 percent in fiscal year 1983−84. The Carter 1982 budget had projected a decline in the rate of growth of defense spending from 17.3 percent to 13 percent in fiscal year 1983−84.

When the spending plans of both administrations are evaluated in constant dollars, a similar pattern of growth is observed. Defense spending in real terms would initially grow (by 10.3 percent) in 1982−83, then decline to 7.9 percent by the end of fiscal year 1984. The Carter budget showed a

Table 3

Reagan Administration Budget Plan in Current Dollars, FY 1981–1984

	Billions of current dollars (est.)				Annual rates of growth (%)		
	1981	1982	1983	1984	1981–82	1982–83	1983–84
I. Spending							
A. Budget projections, FY 82 budget (Carter):							
National defense	161.1	184.4	210.4	237.8	14.5	14.1	13.0
Benefit payments for individuals	319.2	353.4	393.3	431.1	10.7	11.3	9.6
Net interest	67.0	74.8	74.5	72.9	11.6	–0.4	–2.1
Other federal operations	115.5	126.8	139.0	148.5	9.8	9.6	6.8
Total[a]	662.7	739.3	817.3	890.3	11.6	10.6	8.9
B. Budget projections, FY 83 budget (Reagan):							
National defense	159.8	187.5	221.1	253.0	17.3	17.9	14.4
Benefit payments for individuals	316.6	351.6	365.8	385.3	11.1	4.0	5.3
Net interest	68.7	83.0	96.4	98.7	20.8	16.1	2.4
Other federal operations	112.1	103.3	74.3	69.0	–7.9	–28.1	–7.1
Total[a]	657.2	725.3	757.6	805.9	10.4	4.5	6.4

(continued on next page)

Table 3 (continued)
Reagan Administration Budget Plan in Current Dollars, FY 1981–1984

	Billions of current dollars (est.)				Annual rates of growth (%)		
	1981	1982	1983	1984	1981–82	1982–83	1983–84
II. Receipts							
A. Budget projections—Carter administration:							
Individual income taxes	284.0	331.7	384.6	451.2	16.8	16.0	17.3
Corporation income taxes	66.0	64.6	77.6	91.0	−2.1	20.1	17.3
Social insurance tax	184.8	214.7	239.5	264.2	16.2	11.6	10.3
Other	72.7	100.8	107.5	116.0	38.7	6.7	7.9
Total[a]	607.5	711.8	809.2	922.3	17.2	13.7	14.0
B. Budget projections—Reagan administration:							
Individual income tax	285.9	298.6	304.5	322.9	4.4	2.0	6.0
Corporation income tax	61.1	46.8	65.3	83.7	−23.4	39.5	28.2
Social insurance tax	182.7	206.5	222.5	242.5	13.0	7.8	9.0
Other	69.6	74.9	73.8	73.9	7.6	−1.5	0.1
Total[a]	599.3	626.8	666.1	723.0	4.6	6.3	8.5

[a]Totals may not add due to rounding.

Sources: *The Budget of the United States Government*, FY 1982 (Carter administration) and 1983.

Table 4

Reagan Administration Budget Plan in Constant Dollars, FY 1982–1984

	Billions of constant 1972 dollars (est.)				Annual rates of change (%)		
	1981	1982	1983	1984	1981–82	1982–83	1983–84
Budget projections, FY 82 budget—Carter:							
National defense	77.0	80.4	84.4	88.2	4.4	5.0	4.5
Benefit payments for individuals	145.7	145.3	148.2	150.5	−0.3	2.0	1.6
Net interest	17.0	16.1	15.0	13.9	−5.3	−6.8	−7.3
Other federal operations	57.6	58.5	59.0	58.2	1.6	0.9	−1.4
Total[a]	297.3	300.3	306.6	310.7	1.0	2.1	1.3
Budget projections, FY 83 budget—Reagan:							
National defense	76.6	82.6	91.1	98.3	7.8	10.3	7.9
Benefit payments for individuals	163.6	168.6	165.2	166.2	3.1	−2.0	0.6
Net interest	35.5	39.6	43.2	42.1	11.6	9.1	−2.5
Other federal operations	54.9	47.3	31.8	27.9	−13.8	−32.8	−12.3
Total[a]	330.6	338.1	331.3	334.4	2.3	−2.0	0.9

[a]Totals may not add due to rounding.

Sources: *The Budget of the United States Government*, FY 1982 (Carter administration) and 1983.

similar pattern except that the annual rates of growth for
defense were much lower (around 4.5 percent). As to the
overall rate of growth of real spending, the Reagan administration projects a decline from 2.3 percent during 1981–82 to
less than 1 percent real growth by 1984. The Carter budget
projected an increase of about 0.3 percent between 1981–82
and 1983–84.

With respect to budget receipts, further changes have been
proposed. Most of the changes are clearly attributed to the
large reductions in individual and business taxes enacted by
the Reagan administration during fiscal year 1982.

CBO Projections

Unfortunately, it is far from clear that the Reagan projections are realistic. When the president's budget projections
are compared to those made by the Congressional Budget
Office (CBO), one finds substantial difference in the growth
rates of spending and receipts (see tables 5 and 6). The CBO
projects the rate of growth of federal spending for fiscal year
1983–84 to be higher than that projected by the administration (9.9 percent compared to 6.4 percent) and the growth
path for receipts to be lower. The difference between the two
forecasts for budget receipts is quite significant for fiscal
year 1982–83, where the CBO estimates a 3.3 percent
growth rate compared to the administration projection of 6.3
percent. In 1983–84, the CBO projects a rate of growth of
receipts at 7.5 percent compared to the 8.5 percent rate of
growth projected by the administration.

The implication of these projections for the size of the
budget deficit in 1983 and beyond clearly hinges on whose
forecast turns out to be right. Another factor that could
affect the size of future budget deficits has to do with the
New Federalism initiatives of the administration. If the administration's swap proposal were to take effect in fiscal
year 1984, the budget path for 1984–87 might turn out to be
quite different from the path proposed in the 1983 budget.

Table 5
CBO Budget Projections (Baseline), FY 1982–1984

	Billions of current dollars				Annual rates of growth (%)		
	1981	1982	1983	1984	1981–82	1982–83	1983–84
National defense	160	190	214	238	18.7	12.6	11.2
Benefit payments for individuals	320	351	383	413	9.6	9.1	8.1
Net interest	69	85	106	130	23.1	24.7	22.6
Other federal operations	112	113	106	108	0.0	-.6	.2
Total[a]	661	740	809	889	11.2	9.3	9.9
CBO revenue projections (baseline):							
Individual income taxes	285.6	300	303	316	5.2	1.0	4.2
Corporate income taxes	61.1	50	51	62	-18.0	2.0	21.5
Social insurance tax	186.4	209	227	250	12.4	8.6	10.1
Other	69.5	72	71	73	3.5	-1.0	2.8
Total[a]	602.6	631	652	701	4.8	3.3	7.5
CBO reestimates of president's budget deficit:							
President's February budget	57.9	98.6	91.5	82.9	70.3	-7.2	-9.4
CBO budget projections (baseline)	58.4	109.0	157.0	188.0	86.6	44.0	19.8
Deficit with CBO's technical reestimates and baseline economic assumptions	—	111.1	120.6	128.9	—	8.6	6.9

[a]Totals may not add due to rounding.

Sources: *The Budget of the United States Government, FY 1983*, p. M5; CBO, *An Analysis of the President's Budgetary Proposals for Fiscal Year 1983*, prepared at the request of the Senate Committee on Appropriations, February 1982, p. xxi; CBO, *Reducing the Federal Deficit: Strategies and Options*, part III, February 1982.

Table 6
Comparison of Reagan Administration and CBO Budget Assumptions

	1983			1984		
	Reagan	CBO[a] (baseline)	CBO/Reagan	Reagan	CBO[a] (baseline)	CBO/Reagan
GNP						
Current dollars percent change, 4th quarter over 4th quarter	11.0	11.9 *11.1*	+0.9	10.0	10.4 *9.8*	+0.4
Constant dollars (1972) percent change, 4th quarter over 4th quarter	5.2	4.4 *3.0*	−0.8	4.9	3.6 *2.1*	−1.3
GNP deflator Percent change, 4th quarter over 4th quarter	5.5	7.3 *7.9*	+1.8	4.9	6.6 *7.5*	+1.7
CPI Percent change, 4th quarter over 4th quarter	5.1	6.9 *7.6*	+1.8	4.7	6.9 *8.0*	+2.2
Unemployment rate Percent, 4th quarter	7.6	8.0 *8.5*	+0.4	6.8	7.4 *8.4*	+0.6
Interest rate 91-day Treasury bills, percent annual average	10.5	13.2 *14.3*	+2.7	9.5	11.3 *12.7*	+1.8

[a]Numbers in *italics* are CBO "pessimistic alternatives."

Sources: *The Budget of the United States Government, FY 1983*, pp. 2-5 and 2-7; CBO, *An Analysis of the President's Budgetary Proposals for FY 1983*, February 1982, p. 38; CBO, *Reducing the Federal Deficit: Strategies and Options*, February 1982, p. 4.

History of Government Growth and Deficits

It is useful to view the Reagan budget proposals against the historical background of growth in government spending. The record of government growth is not entirely unambiguous. First, it should be noted that when measured in nominal terms, the overall cumulative rate of growth of government spending over the period 1946–1981, although significant, is below the cumulative rate of growth of output. However, rates of growth for some of the spending components are quite staggering. As table 7 shows, the compound growth rates of spending for the purpose of redistributing national income (RS) is around 89 compared to a compounding growth rate for GNP of 13. Of all spending components, the lowest growth rates were those calculated for the nonmarket supply (NS) category.

Second, over the period 1946–1981, a dramatic shift in the public use of resources has taken place, from the provision of nonmarket public goods toward the redistribution, interference with, or distortion of private supply. As shown in table 8, the budget share for nonmarket supply has dropped from 79 percent in 1946 to 33 percent in 1981. The redistributive share rose from 4 percent in 1946 to 34 percent in 1981. Similarly, the share of spending with effects on private supply rose from 7.1 percent in 1946 to 24.8 percent in 1981. A major reallocation seems to have taken place during the 1960s, when the role of government was extended well beyond solving market failures to include modifying market outcomes.

Third, budget deficits are the norm rather than the exception. Since the year 1792, the federal budget has run deficits in 89 years and surpluses in 101 years. Since 1946, the federal budget has shown a deficit in 27 years and surpluses in only 8 years.

Table 7

Annual and Compounding Growth Rates of Output and Government Spending
(in current dollars)

	GNP	Total government expenditures (G)	Nonmarket supply (NS)	Redistribution of private supply (RS)	Modifying-distortion private supply (M-DS)
Annual growth rates[a]					
1946–1981	7.3	6.8	4.8	11.8	9.6
Compounding growth rates[b]					
1946–1981	13.1	9.6	3.4	88.6	36.0
1956–1981	6.0	8.3	3.9	23.4	12.9
1946–1966	2.6	1.8	0.5	10.6	5.0

[a]Calculated by computing $\log x_i = \alpha + B \log T$.
[b]Calculated as follows: $x_{it}/x_{it_o} - 1$.

Source: *The Budget of the United States Government*, several issues.

Table 8
Percentage Distribution of Budget Expenditures by Category, FY 1946–1983[a]

Year	Nonmarket supply (NS)	Redistribution of private supply (RS)	Modifying-distortion private supply (M-DS)
1946	78.9	4.1	7.1
1947	52.6	7.5	25.3
1948	54.2	7.6	23.4
1949	52.8	8.8	27.8
1950	47.2	10.9	32.4
1951	63.4	9.7	19.1
1952	73.4	7.7	14.0
1953	72.7	8.0	13.6
1954	71.1	10.9	11.2
1955	64.3	13.3	15.4
1956	62.6	13.9	16.6
1957	62.9	15.0	15.7
1958	60.1	18.2	15.6
1959	56.9	18.7	19.1
1960	56.1	19.7	17.7
1961	55.8	21.7	16.8
1962	56.3	21.1	17.1
1963	55.9	21.6	16.6
1964	55.6	21.2	17.4
1965	53.4	21.7	18.7
1966	53.1	21.6	19.4
1967	53.4	19.7	21.5
1968	52.6	19.1	23.1
1969	51.1	20.4	22.7
1970	47.6	22.3	24.1
1971	43.9	26.2	24.6
1972	41.5	27.7	25.4
1973	41.0	29.7	25.1
1974	40.0	31.5	24.5
1975	36.8	33.5	24.5
1976	34.0	35.0	25.6
1977	34.3	34.4	25.5

(continued on next page)

Table 8 (continued)
Percentage Distribution of Budget Expenditures by Category, FY 1946–1983[a]

Year	Nonmarket supply (NS)	Redistribution of private supply (RS)	Modifying-distortion private supply (M-DS)
1978	33.4	32.6	27.7
1979	33.5	32.6	27.0
1980	33.0	33.5	26.2
1981	33.1	34.3	24.8
Estimates:[b]			
1982	32.0	34.1	24.5
1983	34.2	34.1	22.0
Averages:			
1946–1981	52.4	20.0	20.7
1950–1960	64.3	13.5	15.8
1960–1970	53.5	21.1	19.8
1970–1981	37.1	31.7	25.5

[a]Categories listed exclude interest payments on the debt. Percentages are for totals including interest.

[b]1982–83 estimates are based on budget numbers reported in the budget for FY 1983 (February 1982).

Source: *The Budget of the United States Government,* several issues.

Why has government grown in this fashion? The growth in the size of the federal government and the continued presence of budget deficits have prompted many to question the wisdom of a budget-making process that sanctions, if not perpetuates, the imbalance between budget outlays and receipts. Although most economists have long agreed that fiscal discipline is needed, during the 1950s and 1960s the notion of balancing the budget was downgraded, as was the use of budget deficits as a fiscal indicator. The actual budget deficit concept was soon replaced by that of full employment deficits; actual balance, by budget balance at full employment.

Table 9
Federal Deficits and Surpluses, 1965–1983

Year	Unified budget Amount (in billions)	Percentage of GNP	Off-budget deficit Amount (in billions)	Percentage of GNP
1965	−1.6	−0.2		
1966	−3.8	−0.5		
1967	−8.7	−1.0		
1968	−25.2	−3.0		
1969	+3.2	0.4		
1970	−2.9	−0.3		
1971	−23.0	−2.2		
1972	−23.4	−2.1		
1973	−14.8	−1.2	−14.9	−1.2
1974	−4.7	−0.3	−6.1	0.4
1975	−45.2	−3.1	−53.2	−3.6
1976	−66.4	−4.1	−73.7	−4.5
1977	−44.9	−2.4	−53.6	−2.9
1978	−48.8	−2.3	−59.2	−2.8
1979	−27.7	−1.2	−49.2	−1.7
1980	−59.6	−2.3	−73.8	−2.9
1981	−57.9	−2.0	−78.9	−2.8
Estimates:				
1982	−108.9	−3.6	−128.2	−4.2
1983	−115.0	−3.4	−129.9	−3.9

Source: *The Budget of the United States Government,* FY 1983. FY 1982–83 estimates taken from OMB, *Current Budget Estimates,* July 1982.

The recent concern over the projected budget path has shifted focus once again from measurements to budget impact. From 1946 to 1981 the ratio of actual budget deficit to GNP seldom amounted to more than 4 percent. In the last 17 years, there has been one year of budget surplus (1969); beyond that, the ratio of deficit to GNP has fluctuated from a low of 0.2 percent in 1965 to a high of 4.1 percent in 1976 (see table 9). Over the next five fiscal years, budget deficits are projected to be well above 5 percent of GNP. Their pattern of increase and decline seems to have merged into only one path—an unabated rise in the ratio of deficit to gross national product.

Measures of the Budget Deficit

It should be emphasized that the current measure of budget deficit, as reported in the National Income and Product Accounts (NIPA), excludes borrowing by off-budget agencies as well as other credit transactions not recorded in the national income accounts, and consequently understates the deficit's true value. On the other hand, one could argue that because the NIPA deficit measurement excludes real gain in the sector net worth, it overstates the size of the deficit.

Another problem with the NIPA measure is that it fails to take account of the autonomous changes in government spending and income due to fluctuations in the level of employment and the inflation rate. Because of these and other shortcomings, alternatives to the NIPA measure have been proposed. Phil Cagan, for example, argues that only the real deficit matters. Accordingly, he has provided us with an estimate of the unified budget deficit *less* the decline in the real value of the stock of debt held outside the Federal Reserve system.[1] Others, including William Niskanen, have argued that the appropriate measure of the budget deficit should take into consideration the net change in the real wealth position and the capital formation activities of the federal sector.[2]

Table 10
Alternative "Suggested" Adjustments for the Federal Budget Deficits, Calendar Years 1970–1980
(in billions of dollars)

	1970	1971	1972	1973	1974	1975	1976	1977	1978	1979	1980
(1) Change in net worth (ΔNW)	−7.9	−14.8	−6.8	7.2	8.1	−56.7	−56.9	−35.8	−13.2	+28.1	−38.7
(2) Depreciation in real value of debt held outside the Federal Reserve system	15.1	15.2	13.7	19.6	32.4	42.6	27.7	35.1	50.2	65.2	79.7
(3) Change in net worth: adjustment (2) + (1)	7.2	.4	6.8	26.8	40.5	−14.1	−29.2	− .7	37.0	93.3	41.0
(4) Inflation premium in interest payments	5.6	5.5	4.4	6.8	12.4	14.9	12.8	12.1	13.4	19.9	23.8
(5) Capital formation in the federal sector	2.8	2.9	3.0	3.1	3.4	4.2	5.5	5.9	7.0	6.7	8.1
(6) Trade balance— surplus or deficit	.5	−3.2	−9.0	−.6	−4.5	11.9	5.1	−13.9	−13.8	−1.7	5.8

Sources: (1) Author's estimates.

(2) Author's estimates. This adjustment corresponds to that of Cagan reported in the *AEI Economist*, November 1981, p. 2, except that Cagan's calculations are for fiscal rather than calendar years.

(4) Determined from estimating the equation: $i = \alpha \cdot \sum_{j=0}^{n} \beta j \, \dot{p}_{t-j} + e$ (where i is the U.S. government bond rate, $\dot{p}_t$ is the inflation rate, and the βj coefficient association with $\dot{p}_{t-j}$ and e is the random disturbance term).

(5) and (6) *Survey of Current Business*, several issues.

Table 10 provides alternative measures of the budget deficit. From the data reported in the table, it is clear that however it is measured, the federal deficit is still sizeable. That is, even after eliminating components attributed to financing capital formation, to autonomous changes in income and spending brought about by fluctuations in the level of economic activity, and/or to the appreciation of the net worth of the federal sector, we still end up with large deficits during the period 1970–1980. This finding suggests that over the past decade the federal government has been withdrawing more resources from the private sector than its income warrants. This reinforces a basic point: what really matters is not so much the size of the deficit as the amount of resources absorbed by the government sector. The question is not of finance, but of use.

There is a great deal of concern regarding projected deficits for fiscal years 1983 through 1987. Since, as we have suggested, one ought not lump together deficits incurred on current accounts and those for the purpose of capital formation, table 11 presents a capital budget for the federal government for fiscal years 1980–83 according to this division.

The data in the table offer valuable insights into the deficit problem. Almost all of the federal budget deficit for 1980–83 occurs on current account, which is an indication that capital formation plays only a minor role in the deficit picture. The data also point the way toward fiscal discipline. Capital budgeting could provide the policymaker with the opportunity to set the accounts straight: in the absence of autonomous changes in outlays and receipts due to fluctuations in economic activity, the federal government should plan for a surplus or, at a minimum, a balance on current account. Budget borrowing would then be used to finance capital accumulation or to rebuild the stock of physical units —a practice that may turn out to be very useful in view of the massive liabilities coming due in the next decade.

Table 11
Capital Budget for the Federal Government
FY 80, 81, 82, 83
(in billions of dollars)

	1980	1981	1982	1983
Current account				
Expenditures:				
Purchases of goods and services	173.7	206.2	235.4	265.5
Defense	135.9	159.8	187.5	221.1
Nondefense	37.9	46.5	47.9	26.5
Transfer payments	242.4	274.6	303.7	315.6
Grants-in-aid to state and local governments	91.5	94.8	91.2	81.4
Interest paid	74.8	83.5	99.6	114.6
Subsidies less surplus government enterprises	6.6	10.6	5.4	−2.1
Depreciation on capital assets	11.3	11.9	13.0	13.3
Total	600.3	681.7	748.3	788.3
Receipts:				
Individual income tax	244.1	285.9	298.6	304.5
Corporate profits tax	64.6	61.1	46.8	65.3
Indirect business tax and nontax receipts	30.0	56.7	60.0	58.0
Social insurance	160.7	182.7	206.5	222.5
Interest received	22.3	15.0	16.6	18.2
Sales of mineral rights	4.1	10.1	7.9	18.0
Total	516.2	600.1	624.5	670.6
Surplus or deficit—current account	−84.1	−81.6	−123.8	−117.7
Capital account				
Purchases of assets:				
Structures	1.4	1.8	1.8	1.7
Equipment	.8	.9	.4	.2
Loans and investments	9.8	5.7	5.4	2.9
Change in commodity inventories	2.3	4.8	1.4	.8
Public works	9.3	10.0	10.8	11.1
Total	23.6	23.2	19.9	16.7

(continued on next page)

Table 11 (continued)
Capital Budget for the Federal Government
FY 80, 81, 82, 83
(in billions of dollars)

	1980	1981	1982	1983
Receipts:				
Loan repayments	1.7	1.8	.4	2.7
Sales of assets	8.0	9.7	11.3	13.2
Transfer from current account for				
depreciation	11.3	11.9	13.0	13.3
Total	21.0	23.4	24.7	29.1
Surplus or deficit—capital account	−2.6	.2	4.8	12.4
Net financial investment	−86.7	−81.4	−119.0	−105.3

Sources: *The Budget of the United States Government,* FY 1982 and 1983; *Special Analysis D,* 1982 and 1983; and Bureau of Economic Analysis.

Deficit Projections

The projected path of the budget deficit for fiscal years 1982–87 is shown in table 12 and figure 1. Figure 2 shows a comparison of the projected paths and actual paths for budget deficits since 1979.

Regardless of who is doing the projections, the deficit picture for the near future does not look overly bright, as seen in table 12. The picture gets bleaker when the administration forecast is discarded in favor of the CBO forecast. Whereas the administration projects a steady decline in the size of the deficit, the CBO shows a reversal of this trend. Rather than falling, the budget deficit was projected in February 1982 to rise from $129 billion in 1982 to something close to $270 billion by 1987. The difference between these two estimates clearly defines what one might want to refer to as the "credibility gap." The size of the gap in 1983 is

Table 12

Projected Federal Deficits, FY 1982–1987[a]
(in billions of dollars)

	1982 (estimated)	1983	1984	1985	1986	1987
GNP current dollars	3160.0	3524.0	3883.0	4258.0	4651.0	5083.0
Deficit CBO baseline projections	−129.0	−176.0	−206.0	−226.0	−254.0	−270.0
% GNP	−4.1	−4.9	−5.3	−5.3	−5.5	−5.3
Deficit Reagan admin., February 1982	−118.3	−107.2	−97.2	−82.8	−77.0	−62.5
% GNP	−3.7	−3.0	−2.5	−1.9	−1.7	−1.2
Deficit Reagan admin., April 1982	−121.4	−117.7	−108.1	−92.8	−85.0	−72.0
% GNP	−3.8	−3.3	−2.8	−2.2	−1.8	−1.4
Deficit Reagan admin., midyear revisions	−218.2	−129.9	−107.0	−85.0	−76.9	−68.3
% GNP	−4.2	−3.9	−2.9	−2.1	−1.7	−1.4

[a]Deficit totals include off-budget outlays.

Sources: *The Budget of the United States Government*, FY 1983, pp. 3-23, 2-5, and 2-7; CBO, *Reducing the Federal Deficit: Strategies and Options*, part III, February 1982, p. 81; OMB, *Midyear Revision*, July 1982, pp. 7, 57.

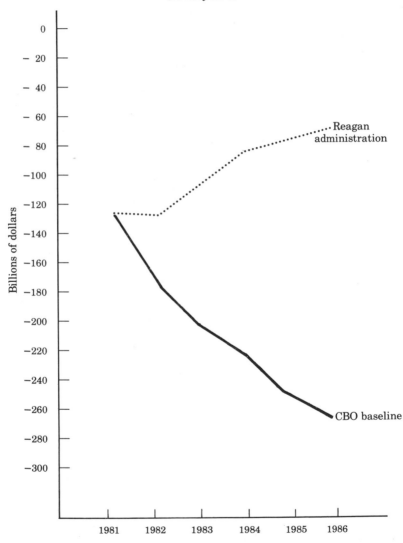

Figure 1

**Projected Deficit, FY 1982–1987:
Reagan Administration
vs.
Congressional Budget Office**

(fiscal years)

Sources: OMB, *Mid-Session Review of the 1982 Budget,* July 1982, p. 57; CBO, *Reducing the Federal Deficit,* 1982, p. 81.

Figure 2
Actual vs. Projected Deficit/Surplus
FY 1979–1987

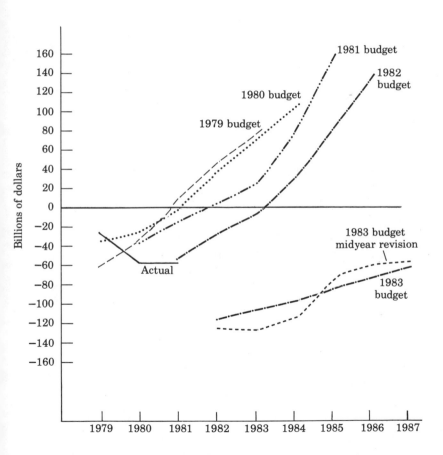

Source: *The Budget of the United States Government,* several issues.

estimated to be about $60 billion. For 1985, this is equal to
$130 billion, and in 1987, it is almost $200 billion.

After allowing for tax increases and spending cuts enacted
in the Omnibus Budget Reconciliation Act of 1982 and the
Tax Equity and Fiscal Responsibility Act of 1982, the CBO
estimated in September 1982 that the growth of the deficit
will be reduced by about one-third, leaving a budget gap
ranging from $150 billion to $180 billion in 1987.

No matter what one might make of these numbers or
which deficit figures are to be believed, it looks as though
budget deficits will remain with us for many years to come.
The question, then, is not so much whether there will be
budget deficits, but rather whether or to what extent the government can exercise budget discipline and control.

Suggestions for Controlling Spending

The government's long record of failure to exercise budgetary discipline regardless of the state of the economy—in recessions as well as during periods of growth—has prompted
many calls for budgetary control either through statutory
remedies or by Constitutional limitations. Such calls reflect
frustration over this proven inability of the federal government to curb its appetite for deficit spending.

Over the past decade, several proposals have been made
for controlling federal spending, including the following:

1. *Cut-and-paste budgeting.* During 1980 and again in 1982,
the Congressional Budget Office was asked to undertake
a study of the possible strategies that could be used to
effect a reduction in the size of the federal budget and/or
the budget deficit. Two reports were issued by the CBO:
Reducing the Federal Budget: Strategies and Examples
(February 1980) and *Reducing the Federal Deficit: Strategies and Options* (February 1982).

The 1980 report offers a smorgasbord of options ranging from outright program reduction or elimination to tax

increases or elimination of tax preferences. The CBO's approach was to identify areas that could lead to budget saving. Areas targeted for budget saving and the cumulative level of saving over the period 1981–85 are as follows:

- Management efficiencies ($6.5 billion).*
- Better targeting ($36.7 billion).
- Shifting responsibilities to state and local governments ($34.6 billion).
- Shifting responsibilities to the private sector ($29.2 billion).
- Revising judgments as to what can be afforded ($88.3 billion).

The CBO strategies for budget reductions would lead to a cumulative budget saving of 4.8 percent of total outlays over the period 1981–85. Of a cumulative budget saving of $195 billion, 45 percent comes from a strategy of "revising judgments as to what can be afforded." The next largest saving, 18.8 percent, is attributed to better program targeting; 17.7 percent of the reduction comes from shifting responsibility to state/local governments; 14.4 percent from shifting responsibility to the private sector; and the residual 3.3 percent from management efficiency.

The rationale behind the CBO strategies seems at first to be both logical and consistent. Better targeting would clearly require management efficiency. Furthermore, it might require shifting responsibilities to state or local governments as well as to individuals. Better targeting might also mean revising our judgment about what can be afforded.

Upon closer inspection, however, this approach is nothing more than cut-and-paste budgeting. There is no reason, without prior knowledge of voters' preferences, why one would want to single out programs such as those

---

*Excluding modification of indexation of entitlement programs.

outlined in the CBO's strategies for cuts or for increases. In addition, although the recommended cuts may illustrate a particular strategy, the specific rationale behind those cuts is unclear and sometimes illogical. Take, for example, the CBO's proposal to terminate certain Social Security benefits. Among the options presented is the elimination of survivors' benefits for parents of children ages 16 and 17, at a savings of $1.7 billion over the years 1981–85. One might ask what kind of logic would dictate such a change. Why the age of 16 in view of the present limit of 18?

Another example is the elimination of the general revenue-sharing program. This program change would result in a five-year saving of $14.6 billion. The CBO's reason for the elimination is the fact that "revenue sharing payments to state governments have been steadily declining in real terms and thus their elimination would have only a small overall impact on the financial position of state governments." The point, however, is not whether revenue sharing makes up a decreasing proportion of state and local government budgets; rather, such a cut should be made if the program is no longer efficient or desirable.

Other examples can be found in the report to reinforce the point that Congress should not settle for this kind of budgeting. In a representative democracy, budget allocations as well as budget adjustments to those allocations should reflect constituents' preferences and not be based merely on someone's arbitrary judgment. The strategies proposed by the CBO clearly do not reflect the preferences of the electorate; instead, they are shaped by the values as well as the analytical judgments of CBO staff.

2. *Statutory remedies.* Another approach to budget controllability would rely on statutory remedies to improve the Congressional budget process. In a forthcoming volume

entitled *Constraining Federal Taxing and Spending,* Allen Schick lists four conditions for budget control:[3]

- Congress should fix the size of the budget before allocating shares among federal committees. Basic to this condition is that once reached, the decision would not be easily reversed.

- Functional allocations should be binding upon Congress. That is, to effect controllability of the total, the budget allocations must first be controlled.

- The quality of economic projections should be improved so that biases, especially on the revenue side of the budget, would not make it easier for Congress to forego controllability.

- Perhaps most importantly, indexation of so-called "uncontrollable" programs should be discontinued. These programs must be subjected to the same competitive pressures for the budget dollar as are discretionary claims.

Congress' failure to control spending is not for lack of budget tools; rather, it is due to a lack of willpower. In short, although Congress can pass laws designed to control spending or to create a mechanism for control, thus far it has not been able to do so. Because conventional remedies seem to have failed, current hopes often rest with some form of Constitutional limit.

3. *Spending limitations amendments.* Perhaps the most widely discussed of these limits is S.J. Res. 58, the balanced budget/tax limitation Constitutional amendment. The major provisions of this amendment are:

- Actual outlays (where outlays include all those except for the repayment of the national debt) may not exceed budgeted outlays.

- Budgeted outlays may not exceed budgeted receipts (all receipts except those derived from borrowing);

but this may be waived by a three-fifths majority in both houses.

- Budgeted receipts may not grow proportionately faster than national income. This may be waived by a simple majority of all members of both houses.
- States may not be forced to shoulder federal programs without full federal compensation.
- The amendment is waived in case of war.

The first difficulty with the amendment is that it may bind us to a level of receipts as a share of national income that is too high (or perhaps even too low). The amendment would in fact set the ratio of taxes to GNP at whatever the rate was at the time the amendment became effective, with only minor variations occurring thereafter. Yet projections have shown the time path of this ratio to differ greatly, depending on whether the amendment became effective in 1978 or 1983.

The second difficulty with S.J. Res. 58 has to do with its impact on congressional allocation among individual programs. Because the amendment presses Congress to control spending aggregates or the rate of growth of those aggregates and says nothing about individual spending components, there is no guarantee that adjustments to these components will turn out to be optimal. Put differently, because the rates of growth of federal programs and the political power behind them are not uniform, Congress may find it easier to make across-the-board adjustments for all spending programs rather than face up to the much more difficult task of effecting differential cuts. Constitutional limits on aggregate spending may give Congress a way out of its current dilemma of how to deal with competing claims on the budget dollar; but the cost will be to sound, responsible budgeting.

Concluding Remarks

The outlook for a balanced budget, at least in the near future, is not bright. The budget shortfall for 1983–84 is around 2.8 percent of GNP; for 1985 and beyond it is in the neighborhood of 5 percent.

There are few options for balancing the federal budget. One is to effect an across-the-board cut in all federal programs to bring the federal budget's share of GNP from the 22.1 percent projected for 1983 to 19.3 percent, and from the 21.2 percent projected for 1984 to 18.4 percent. Another is to enact tax increases and/or selective spending reductions.

Since submitting its February budget, the Reagan administration has been looking for ways to reduce the projected deficit. The option finally adopted involves a program of tax increases and spending reductions. The Tax Equity and Fiscal Responsibility Act of 1982 adopted by Congress would raise revenues by $100 billion and cut spending by $17 billion in fiscal years 1983–85. And the recently passed Omnibus Budget Reconciliation Act of 1982 calls for an additional $13 billion reduction in outlays over the same years. These two actions are expected to reduce budget deficits for 1983–85 to around $155 billion annually, considerably less than earlier forecasts but a far cry from a balanced budget.

RESPONSE

Peggy B. Musgrave: "The Need for Precision"

Let me say at the outset that I like Professor Ott's general approach and methodology. Rather than advocating sweeping constraints (which could result in subsequent inefficiencies in resource allocation when out of line with public preferences regarding the level and mix of public services), Professor Ott has searched for the reasons for and the sources of the increased role of the federal government in the economy, which may give a clue to the appropriate action needed. This is an approach I prefer to the sweeping assumption that the growth of government expenditures relative to GNP is a reflection of a bureaucracy run wild, an assumption that calls for radical prescriptions such as Constitutional limitations.

With regard to the experience of the recent past, I might add the following point. Because of the growing interdependence of federal, state, and local governments, it would seem appropriate to begin by considering the consolidated expenditures of all levels of government in relation to GNP. Since 1950, the general rule has been for this ratio to rise by three percentage points each decade. Until the early 1970s this increase was two-thirds federal, but in the last decade it has been two-thirds state-local. Thus recent acceleration in the growth of government expenditures relative to GNP has been at the state-local rather than the federal level. Moreover, I am referring to self-financed expenditures at the state-local level, where grass-roots democracy is often thought to have its strongest expression.

As to the composition of federal expenditures, it is clear that only defense and transfer payments really matter. Federal purchases of civilian goods and services were only

1.6 percent of GNP in 1950 and are only 2.4 percent thereof today. And with the steady decline of defense expenditures since the early 1960s, total federal purchases declined as a percentage of GNP from 10.6 percent in 1960 to 7.0 percent in 1979. As Professor Ott points out, it is to federal transfer payments that one must turn for an explanation of the sources and causes of the upward creep of federal expenditures as a share of national income. And, I might add, the lion's share of that upward creep has been accounted for by the social insurance programs.

Let us turn now to a consideration of the need for control. While it is always desirable and necessary that federal expenditure programs be regularly subject to review and evaluation and that high standards of efficiency be required, increases in the share of government expenditures in the economy should not be rejected out of hand. It is not surprising that a growing population density, technological changes, and industrial development over time help to create the kinds of externalities that require remedial government intervention. Governmental activity reflects growing interdependencies and the impinging of groups one upon another. Furthermore, it is not difficult to see why many of the goods and services provided through government should be complementary to leisure-related activities that tend to be highly elastic. And I venture to suggest that the major sources of expenditure growth, namely transfer payments and social insurance programs, have reflected changing social values over time. These social values, to be sure, are subject to reversal as political climates change, as we see in this country at the present time. But it does not seem to me that we should seek to put controls on public preferences for government expenditures, preferences that by all accounts are subject to change from one generation to another. Implementation of those preferences is, after all, what democracy is all about. This is not to say that expenditure programs should not be carefully scrutinized from time to time, and structural

changes may be called for. This may well be the case for the
Social Security system, which has been the major component
of growth. It is probable that the Social Security system
should be brought into better balance between the interests
of the contributing and retired generations, and that the
working generation should not be expected to carry all the
burdens imposed by changing demographics and produc-
tivities. Beyond that, I would suggest that increases in other
types of social transfer payments are to be expected and accepted as our society implements the call for equal opportunities arising from the various civil rights movements of
the 1960s. A true conservative, it seems to me, would
vigorously support the promotion of equal economic opportunities, albeit opposing a progressive income tax.

No sensible person, of course, can be pleased with the way
in which the problems of welfare and relief of poverty have
been and are being dealt with. Obviously work opportunities
are better than welfare for those able to work, but putting
this into practice, as all experts agree, would be more rather
than less expensive compared with what is now done.

One of the messages of Professor Ott's paper, a correct one
I think, is that one cannot propose putting constraints on the
growth of federal government without taking a disaggregated approach and looking at the proper role for the federal
government on the one hand and the various expenditure
categories on the other. Federal budgetary activity involves
three dimensions—the overall size of the budget, the composition of that budget, and the degree of budget balance.
The overall level should be determined not only by the "correct" division between public and private resource claims but
also by the proper division between federal on the one hand
and state-local expenditure responsibilities on the other. Increasing economic and social interdependencies have called
forth ever more intertwined and complex relationships
among the three levels of government. Turning back the
clock to a simpler and less fiscally interdependent era is not

possible. Thus, constraints on the growth of federal expenditures must be seen within this broader pattern of intergovernmental fiscal relations. There is a certain inescapable logic to the assignment of particular expenditure functions and revenue-raising responsibilities to each level of government, as the recent retreat over the "New Federalism" has shown.

There is another very important point to be made with respect to controls over federal spending. A system of budget procedures is needed that will allow changes in direction of one of the three dimensions (level, composition, and balance of the federal budget) to be made without distorting and upsetting objectives with respect to the others. The recent experience with Reaganomics has provided a classic example for the textbooks of how poorly our system works in this respect. Motivated largely by a desire to put pressure on Congress to reduce the level of federal expenditures, the administration pushed through a program of tax reduction that later proved to have dire consequences for the budget deficits of future years, forcing an overreliance on monetary policy. This process of bringing about budgetary contraction makes no more sense than the budgetary expansion of earlier administrations unaccompanied by adequate financing provision.

I cannot agree that the soaring size of projected deficits in both absolute and relative terms is evidence of an uncontrollable budget. It results from a deliberate, discretionary policy action to reduce taxes and raise defense expenditures. Rather, one might say it is taxes that have run wild in a downward direction as the way has been opened for a wide range of special interest tax expenditures on top of the administration's rate reductions. Before moving to more radical means of control, better ways should be sought for linking financing arrangements with expenditure increase or expenditure consequences with tax reduction. Taxes and expenditures should be decided upon in unison. The fact that in large measure they are not is a grave shortcoming of our budgetary process.

Cutting back the level of federal expenditures by across-the-board reductions is also in my opinion a poor way of bringing about a reduced role for government, for it may sacrifice correct decisions with respect to the composition of the budget. It offends both the entire notion of efficiency at the margin and the proposition that reductions no less than increases in expenditures should pass the test of cost-benefit analysis. I am surprised that an administration that has placed such strong emphasis on the importance of efficiency in resource allocation as it applies to public/private sector relationships should have overlooked this consideration in proposing budget cutbacks that largely ignore efficiency criteria in determination of the budget composition.

6

RICHARD A. MUSGRAVE

The Reagan Administration's Fiscal Policy: A Critique

It is painfully evident that the Reagan administration's macroeconomic policy has been a failure. While the inflation rate has come down, this reduction has been accompanied by heavy unemployment, now exceeding 10 percent, with loss of output and with an inequitable distribution of the economic burden. To make matters worse, the administration's lopsided combination of tight money and fiscal ease has lifted real interest rates to record levels, thereby defeating its very objective of an investment- and growth-based recovery. The record, as I see it, far from demonstrates the much-touted

failure of mainstream economics. On the contrary, mainstream economics told us from the beginning that so ill-
designed a program would have to fail. Bad economics, based
on wishful thinking, has produced bad results. The administration's eagerness to install structural changes while its political clout was strong is understandable; but this should not
have been permitted to override the formulation of a sound
policy for dealing with the immediate issues of stabilization.
Here the administration has earned a failing grade on most
counts. How its longer-run objectives will work out remains
to be seen. The sharp cutback in the nondefense public sector, the reduced marginal tax rates, the moves toward fiscal
decentralization—these issues involve not merely economic
considerations, but also broad social considerations to which
I will return shortly.

Stabilization and Macroeconomic Policy

I begin with the immediate economic issues of stabilization
and macroeconomic policy. According to the administration's
early promises as presented in its initial messages, a fiscal
policy of tax and expenditure cuts combined with a reduced
growth rate of M_1 would tame inflation without much pain,
restore economic health, and balance the budget by 1984.
Such would be the case even though the administration's tax
cut of $184 billion, increased defense of $78 billion, and nondefense cuts of $122 billion would add to a potential increase
in deficit of $122 billion at 1984 levels. But this would be
more than offset by built-in revenue gains as the economy
returned to high employment, thereby balancing the budget
by 1984. While in the tax legislation of 1981, Congress essentially adopted the administration's recommendation, the
forecast went wrong in two respects. For one thing, cutbacks
in nondefense programs (whatever their substantive merit)
proved infeasible on the scale proposed; moreover, additional
outlays arose through rising interest and recession effects.

For another, the expected built-in revenue gain turned into losses as the anticipated recovery was replaced by a deepening recession. As a result, the promise of a balanced budget by 1984 soon yielded to the prospect of ever-rising deficits. The deficit now expected for 1983 ranges around $125 billion, and rising deficits and deficit-to-GNP ratios may be expected in the mid-1980s. Such, at least, will be the case unless a substantial revision in policy occurs.

As should have been evident from the beginning, the administration's 1981 scenario was wholly unrealistic. The called-for reduction in the growth rate of M_1 was incompatible with the projected rise in GNP, absent a sensational speedup in velocity. As could be expected, tight money did its job, depressing the economy and deepening the recession as well as curtailing inflation. The assumed early response of the private sector to the tax cut was equally unrealistic, as was the assumption that favorable expectations would stem the upward pressure on interest rates generated by tight money. Expectations indeed played a key role, but in a direction opposite from that desired. The prospect of continuing deficits was translated into expectations of continuing inflation, following, ironically, the logic of the president's campaign argument that government deficits are indeed *the* source of inflation. Thereby long- as well as short-term real interest rates were pushed to record-breaking levels.

As an experiment in the contemporary history of thought, it is interesting to observe the changing array of economic theories that have been offered in support of administration policy. Central to the administration's early forecast was the proposition that the tax cut would generate an early and massive economic expansion. This expansion would be based not on the multiplier-accelerator mechanism of mainstream economics but on "supply-side" effects. Reduced tax rates would increase net rates of return and thereby operate to raise work effort and investment. According to its earlier and more extreme Kemp-Roth or Laffer version, the cut in rates and resulting rise in base might even increase yield. Of course, the idea of a maximum revenue rate—embodied in the so-called "Laffer Curve"—was nothing new, as reference to any standard public finance text will show. What was new was the contention that existing rates were in fact beyond that point, and that the supply response would come about almost at once. This was wishful thinking. Economists may debate the potential favorable supply-side effects of tax reduction over the long run, but they should agree that these effects could not possibly be realized within a year or two. Changes in labor supply do not come about overnight; and changes in productivity generated by an increased capital stock clearly take years to accumulate. Moreover, even if tax reduction were to generate a prompt increase in investment, the resulting increase in supply would also generate a corresponding rise in income and demand, leaving the level of excess demand unaffected. A favorable effect on inflation comes about only when an increased capital stock generates productivity growth, and this takes time. The supply-side case for tax reduction sans deficit is thus untenable, at least over the short run; and the Keynesian mechanism of demand creation cannot operate if offset by tight money.

Bizarre though it may seem, an administration that deplores deficits thus set out on a course of massive deficit creation. Faced with the reality of large and rising deficits, the administration presented various arguments to show that deficits after all do not matter, provided only that they are financed without supporting monetary expansion. First came the argument that such financing would be possible without pressure on interest rates, because the resulting increase in income and private savings would suffice to absorb the debt. In the Keynesian context, this is hardly possible. If the increase in disposable income due to tax reduction flowed into savings that in turn were absorbed by public debt, the rate of interest would be unchanged, but so would be the level of pretax income. The burden of the argument once more falls on short-term supply-side effects.

Next there came the more sophisticated proposition that the choice between tax and loan finance does not matter (i.e., fiscal policy is neutral) because consumers, well versed in the economics of superrational expectations, would respond equally to either form of finance. They would capitalize the present value of future tax obligations, so that their net worth would be reduced equally in both cases. While elegant in concept, this is, in my view, a wholly unrealistic reading of household responses, at least in the short run. Finally, there was a proposition, political rather than economic in nature, that tax cuts would not produce deficits because Congress, abhorring deficits, would cut expenditures accordingly. But would it? As noted below, the tax cut has added to the pressure for reducing civilian programs, but the magnitudes of these cuts have fallen far short of the deficit-generating forces of the administration's tax cut and defense increase.

In all this, it is of course essential to distinguish between deficits that come about as a built-in response of the fiscal system to recession, and deficits that result from tax rate reduction or new expenditure legislation. Such is the well-known difference between a change in current and in "full-employment" deficits. This essential analytical distinction, I regret to say, appears to have been dropped from the pages of the last official *Economic Report*. Of course, there is nothing wrong with generating a substantial built-in deficit when unemployment runs at close to 10 percent. My complaint is not that aggregate demand policy as a whole has been too easy. Indeed, too much reliance has been placed on curing inflation cold turkey, with insufficient regard for the economic and human costs of deepening recession. Acceptance of a moderate form of income policy would have reduced that cost. What *is* troublesome is that (1) we would have been better off with a smaller deficit matched by easier money, and (2) the administration's fiscal design has created the prospect of large full-employment deficits in the mid-1980s, at a time when unemployment will presumably be reduced to

acceptable levels. Fiscal policy will then be too loose for
stability, certainly so unless tight money becomes even
tighter, stifling investment and productivity growth. The administration's reversal in supporting tax increase legislation
in 1982 has helped matters somewhat, but the resulting
revenue gain remains far short of the loss introduced under
the 1981 act.

While our concern here is with the administration's fiscal
program, tight money is so intrinsic a part of the scheme that
it cannot be overlooked entirely. Given the administration's
tax cut—based program of fiscal ease, the entire burden of
restraint was placed on the Fed, making it hardly fair now to
blame the Fed for trying to carry out its assigned role. To be
sure, installing a steady growth path of M_1 proved more
difficult than monetarist doctrine had assumed—as we all
know, the greatest danger to one's pet theory is to have it
tried. But I find it very unconvincing to argue that all would
have been well if the trend line of M_1 growth had been held
steady. The main point is that monetary growth has been
slowed and the expected consequences have come about. My
quarrel with Federal Reserve policy rather would be directed
at excessive concern with M_1 as distinct from interest rates,
the credit volume, and economic conditions. Also I would
have thought that some concern with selective controls
would have been helpful, especially since it is evident that
general monetary tightness results in a highly uneven impact on various sectors of the economy.

However, this is not our theme here.

The Runaway Budget

I now leave the general aspects of macroeconomic policy and
turn to the administration's stand on the federal budget. On
the expenditure side, the administration's central tenet is
that the budget is out of control. Expanding at an ever-
increasing rate and driven by the greed of its bureaucrats, it

is about to swallow the American economy and deprive us of our traditional liberties. To deal with this threat, while at the same time making room for a sharp expansion of defense outlays, a drastic curtailment in nondefense spending is said to be imperative. Given the difficulty of curtailing entitlement programs including, as we are now assured, Social Security commitments, the burden of shrinkage must fall on the remaining and flexible parts of the nondefense budget, including mainly welfare and a set of smaller social programs. All this can be done, so the argument goes, while preserving a safety net for the truly needy. By thus shifting resources from what are considered unproductive uses in the public to productive uses in the private sector, our economy is to gain new vigor and our freedom is to be increased.

But let us take a closer look at the administration's case. I begin with the president's favorite characterization of the budget as reflecting a runaway and hemorrhaging condition. The fact of the matter is that the federal budget, as a percentage of GNP, rose from 18.3 percent in 1960 to 20.5 percent in 1970 and 21.1 percent in 1979. While the budget has expanded in relation to GNP, the expansion has hardly been violent and has in fact occurred at a declining rate. Note also that the ratio of federal government purchases to GNP declined from 10.6 percent in 1960 to 7.0 percent in 1979, thus reducing the federal government's actual share in direct resource use. Federal employment as a share in total employment similarly declined. The increase in expenditures can be accounted for almost entirely by the growth in transfer payments—mainly Social Security, welfare, and medical programs. These transfers did not involve a direct public resource use, but rather a shift of funds from one part of the private sector to another. This does not mean that such programs are without social costs, but the resulting displacement of market decisions was much less than is implied in the administration's sweeping claim that government oversight has replaced private choice. Looking at the past two decades, one can hardly conclude that they reflected an explosive trend of expenditure growth. Nor can it be argued that budget deficits during this period were *the* or even *a* major source of inflation. Nonbudgetary factors were of prime importance, and credit growth due to absorption of public debt was only a small part of total monetary expansion. Household deficits, in the form of consumer credit, were of much larger importance.

Expenditure growth accelerated over 1979–1981, when as a ratio of GNP government expenditure rose from 21 to 23 percent. That growth was a reflection of the compounded impact of recession and inflation, as well as of the accelerated growth of certain programs such as student loans and Medicaid. These developments, to be sure, are a matter of concern, and there is good reason, especially at this time, to guard against programs that are not worth their cost. But this is a far cry from the administration's strategy of first installing a tax cut, then requiring a sharp defense increase, and finally making nondefense program cuts the residual item that has to be adjusted to close the self-created gap.

As I have argued for a long time, adjustments in the budget needed as a matter of stabilization policy should be made on the revenue rather than the expenditure side. Under conditions of inflation, this requires higher rather than lower rates of tax. The level of public programs in turn should be determined on the basis of their worth. Last year's performance in the so-called budget reconciliation was anything but a prudent review of expenditure needs, and the present state of the budget discussion looks little better. As has been pointed out by the Congressional Budget Office and other sources, the administration's plan, or the legislation enacted under the threat of its veto power, has involved redistribution from the bottom up. Combined with reliance on heavy unemployment as an inflation cure, this has favored the well-to-do while hurting the poor. If in the process the spillover of some social programs to middle-income and higher-income families has been curtailed, that is all to the good. But much of the cutback has fallen on essential social programs such as CETA (Comprehensive Employment and Training Act), food supplements for mothers and children, handicapped student programs, food stamps, child nutrition, and so forth. It seems neither efficient nor right to cut back these programs in order to permit massive tax reductions whose benefits accrue largely toward the upper-income range. It is simply incorrect to view the looming deficits of the mid-1980s as a consequence of a runaway nondefense budget. These deficits are the consequence of rising defense combined with mounting revenue losses due to the administration's strategy of tax reduction.

We do not here have the time to analyze detailed cutbacks or program repeals. What matters is the principle by which expenditure revision should proceed. The starting point should not be a presumption — as suggested by President Reagan's demeaning references to the public sector — that public programs are useless while private uses of funds are productive. Rather, alternative uses of funds and resources should be weighed against each other at the margin. Undoubtedly, this leaves much the larger share of resource use in private hands, but public uses, over the relevant range, are essential as well to the functioning of a fair society and indeed of the private sector. There are many things that a market economy, left to its own devices, can do, but it cannot do all. Certain services must be paid for through the budget, and externalities occurring in the conduct of private affairs must be corrected for. Moreover, one need not be an egalitarian to observe that some deficiencies in the distribution of income need to be corrected, if not as a matter of social decency then as a political safeguard to render an essentially private-enterprise economy viable in our time. Income support programs should be designed so as to avoid abuse. Where abuse does occur it should be corrected, and failure to do so may have contributed greatly to reduced acceptance of such programs. At the same time, it should be kept in mind that the ultimate remedy for economic disadvantage can lie only in providing adequate work opportunities for all—the very opposite of what is now being done by running a depressed economy. The administration's contention that matters of welfare can be taken care of by private charity is neither realistic nor to me acceptable. A fair and democratic society should be organized so that people are entitled to the opportunity of making a decent living—entitled to this opportunity and not dependent upon the charity of others. Together with this recognition goes the notion that a citizen should be proud to pay his or her taxes. "Taxes," as Justice Holmes well put it, "are the price of civilization," and not— as has been suggested by some—a badge of slavery. This might be considered a shocking statement in the year 1982, but I hope that America someday will come back to this point of view.

Let me add a word about proposals to implant a budget limitation amendment in the federal Constitution. While such an amendment has not been the primary target of the Reagan program, it has the administration's support, absurd as this may seem while we move into a period of record deficits. Such an amendment would hamstring the operation of stabilization policy and would not solve our problems. Improvement in budgetary procedure to assure prudent legislation and to make clear that public programs have an opportunity cost is all to the good. But to freeze the expenditure share by Constitutional amendment in response to the political sentiments of a particular Congress is not the way to conduct business in a democratic society. Freedom of choice should apply no less to the selection of public services than to the selection of chewing gum.

Tax Policy

I now turn to the administration's tax policy. This policy, as enacted in the revenue legislation of 1981, provided for a three-stage income tax cut of 5, 10, and 10 percent in 1981, 1982, and 1983 respectively. It also provided for a massive corporation tax cut through speeding up of depreciation. In addition, there was a substantial easing of the estate tax. It is only fair to add that these changes, while proposed or supported by the administration, also enjoyed broad bipartisan congressional support. A critique of this legislation, therefore, is addressed as much to Congress, in particular to the Democratic leadership of the Ways and Means Committee, as it is to the administration.

The income tax cut, implementing the Kemp-Roth proposal, involved a more or less flat across-the-board percentage cut in rates, with the exception of the top, where marginal rates on earned income were cut to 50 percent. From the standpoint of macroeconomic policy, the introduction of a three-year tax cut schedule was unfortunate, as is now evidenced by the deficit prospects for 1983 and beyond. I do not have much quarrel with how the cut was structured, except that I would have liked to have seen somewhat more substantial relief at the lower end. This could have been done, at little revenue cost, by increasing the standard deduction. My main concern in the field of income tax legislation is with the introduction of inefficient and useless new tax expenditures, as illustrated most strikingly by the All-Savers Certificates. At the same time, I should record my approval of the indexing provision that is to go into effect in 1985. While this may require rate increases or spoil the possibility of nominal rate reductions, indexing is necessary to preserve or restore the integrity of the income tax. My view here differs with that of some of my colleagues whose perspective on tax matters I otherwise share.

However this may be, major administration proposals for income tax reform are still pending. While various suggestions have come from the White House—such as that progressive taxation is immoral (Counselor Meese) or that the proposal for a broad-based flat-rate income tax is attractive

(the president)—specific proposals have yet to come. I am of
course delighted with any move towards base broadening
and the resulting possibility of rate reduction. This is exactly
what I have been proposing for decades. But it is a non se-
quitur to conclude that such rate reduction has to be linked
with transition to a flat rate that combines rate reduction at
the upper to middle with rate increases at the lower end of
the scale. I am worried that we may end up with a flat rate
while retaining gaps in the base—e.g., tax exemptions, imperfect inclusion of capital gains, mortgage interest deduction—the main benefit of which accrues over the middle-
and upper-income range. Keep in mind that the income tax is
the progressive component in an otherwise largely regressive
tax structure, so that with a flat income tax the overall
system could readily become regressive. To be sure, even a
flat-rate income tax results in a progressive effective rate
over the lower half of the income range, due to exemptions
and the standard deduction, but progressive bracket rates
are needed to maintain a meaningful degree of progression
over the upper end of the scale. Far from considering this immoral, I consider it appropriate for a democratic society that
a modest degree of progression should apply over the upper
range. In all, I do not accept the link to a flat (rather than
reduced) rate structure that some of the proposals seem to
imply, but I am delighted to find the idea of a broad tax base
to have unexpectedly reemerged, especially in view of the
rather befuddled discussion of tax expenditures in the administration's recent budget. Some of the changes introduced in the Revenue Act of 1982 make a good beginning.

Let me now turn to the corporate relief provided by the
1981 legislation. The essence of this legislation was to replace the Asset Depreciation Range system (ADR) with the
new Accelerated Cost Recovery System (ACRS). Properties
are now classified into four groups, with depreciation periods
of 15, 10, 5, and 3 years respectively; most eligible equipment
property is in the five-year and real estate in the ten-year

class. There are three objections to the ACRS. First, there had been general agreement that something needed to be done to protect the depreciation base against inflation, but the ACRS does not do so in an adequate fashion. The best way of immunizing the real value of depreciation against inflation would have been to index the base. Alternatively, to achieve essentially the same result, Congress might have adopted the Jorgenson-Auerbach plan of first-year depreciation. This plan would have placed the entire depreciation deduction in the first year, thus eliminating the impact of inflation but doing so at a value equal to the present value of economic depreciation in the absence of inflation. It would have neutralized inflation, independent of changing inflation rates. But the ACRS does not. By shortening asset lives, it takes a step toward immunizing the system against inflation, but the effective tax rate will still rise and fall with the inflation rate, especially for longer-lived assets.

Secondly, the shortening of asset lives under the ACRS in combination with the investment credit will result in wide differentials in effective rates. Recent estimates for 1986 (when the provisions will be fully effective) show a rate of −47% for three-year assets, −39% for five-year assets, and +40% for industrial buildings. Similar estimates shown in somewhat involuted form in this year's *Economic Report* record the pretax rates of return needed to yield a 4% after-tax return. For 1986, these range from 2.2% for construction machinery to 6.3% for industrial buildings, suggesting effective rates varying from −82% to +37%. For an administration that places such emphasis on not interfering with market choices, this is indeed a strange system. The efficiency costs of resulting distortions in investment decisions will go far to cancel or outweigh whatever gain in growth may result from granting the incentive. One wonders how so disturbing a piece of legislation could have been proposed and could have passed the scrutiny of Congress.

Thirdly, because of the interaction of accelerated deprecia-

tion and investment credits, the new ACRS system results in
high levels of *negative* rates of tax. As noted before, the corporation tax on earnings from depreciable assets of short and
medium lives will be not only eliminated but turned into a
heavily negative rate—i.e., a negative income tax for corporations. To this were added the liberalized leasing provisions that in effect permit unused credits to be traded,
thereby assuring that low and negative tax rates will be
realized. Some of the excesses of the 1981 legislation have
now been reversed by the 1982 law, but much remains to be
done to establish an inflation-neutral and less discriminatory system.

While I have argued above that the supply-side aspects of
taxation effects are of little relevance to shorter-run stabilization policy, they do pose relevant issues in the longer-run
context of economic growth. There is a presumption that increased emphasis on efficiency and incentive considerations
may conflict with the idea of progressive taxation. It cannot
be disputed that, counting Pareto efficiency only, the best of
all taxes is a head or lump-sum tax. But it is also evident that
such a tax system is unacceptable in the real world, which
(happily) demands that issues of equity also be allowed for.
The problem then is (1) to design incentive measures so as to
minimize interference with equity, and (2) having done so, to
use good judgment regarding the desirable trade-off of
weights between efficiency and equity. Point (2) may be
largely a matter of personal values, but point (1) is open to
economic analysis. The first and most obvious step should be
to correct aspects of the law that are undesirable on both
equity and incentive grounds, e.g., some of the major tax
preferences now included in the income tax. Having done so,
the next move is to design incentives in line with the equity
constraint. I find little in the 1981 legislation that fits this
pattern and much that is in flagrant contradiction to it. The
current proposals of a broad base, however, offer a hopeful
perspective, and parts of the 1982 legislation offer a step in
the right direction.

The New Federalism

There remains a final dimension of the administration's fiscal program: its call for a new and less centralized form of fiscal federalism. The president's 1981 and 1982 budgets called for continued consolidation of categorical grants into block grants, a program already begun under the Nixon administration. The major proposal, however, appeared only in the Budget Message of 1983. It would have the federal government assume full responsibility for Medicaid, while the states would assume full responsibility for AFDC (Aid to Families with Dependent Children) and food stamp programs. Also, the responsibility for forty-eight other grant programs would be returned to the states by 1988. In the meantime, special financing through a trust fund would be arranged, but the states would not be required to use their proceeds for specific programs. After 1988, the federal government would vacate some revenue sources to the states, so as to compensate them for the loss of grants.

The view of federalism that underlies these changes is that public sector functions are performed better at the state and local level than by the federal government. The U.S. citizen essentially is a citizen of his/her state, with matters of defense and foreign policy delegated to the federation. Beyond this, it should not be a federal responsibility to assure that people living in various states are provided with an adequate level of public services. Nor should it be a federal responsibility to worry about the fact that various jurisdictions differ greatly in tax bases and needs, and hence in the tax effort required to provide such services. This approaches a Jeffersonian view of fiscal federalism, but the question is whether such a view is tenable 200 years later and, one might add, whether Jefferson himself would advance it at this time. After all, adherence to an idyllic society of small rural communities would demand the repeal not only of large government but also of large corporations, modern industry, banking, and indeed most features of modern life.

In today's United States, there exists a high degree of mobility in commerce and population, yielding a unitary market to which much of the success of the American economy may be traced. Because of this integration, common policies on matters such as wars, defense, immigration, and business cycles affect all of us, but their regional impacts differ. It is only fair, therefore, that the consequences of joint policies be borne jointly. Many of the fiscal problems of our older cities, for instance, are a consequence of national policies, such as failure to deal with unemployment and attitudes toward immigration—issues that are of national origin and that require national concern. I see no reason why taxpayers in upstate New York should have to share in the costs of reconstructing the Bronx any more than taxpayers in, say, Utah. We are all citizens of these United States and responsible for its policies.

Moreover, it should not be assumed too easily that fiscal decentralization is always efficient. Decentralization, to be sure, may be efficient in that it permits various jurisdictions to differ in their provision of social goods, and in line with their particular preferences. But substantial differences in the levels and structure of state taxation also affect the movement of economic resources and distort efficiency in location. State tax differentials are not unlike tariffs and provide the same interference with free trade. Decentralized fiscal systems therefore are harmless only if they are more or less equalized, in which case the very advantage of decentralization is lost; or they are harmless if the public sector is small, so that differentials do not matter.

Similar considerations hold with regard to the income distribution aspects of fiscal policy. As I have argued for a long time, redistribution policies must be central to be effective. If regionally based, they will simply result in the movement of high-income taxpayers out of, and low-income taxpayers into, progressive tax jurisdictions, thereby voiding the objectives of redistribution. It is only natural, therefore, that progressive taxes are largely used at the central level, in the U.S. as elsewhere, while state taxes tend to be regressive. This being the case, fiscal decentralization means a shift in the overall tax structure towards a less progressive system. This is precisely what we are now experiencing, and that may well be one of the reasons why the New Federalism is being proposed. Add to this that the shift from categorical to block grants will result in the displacement of programs for people with low incomes, and the tendency toward upward redistribution in the administration's general approach again becomes apparent.

By raising these considerations, I do not mean to deny that the traditional system of categorical grants may have imposed too many specific restrictions on spending, and that greater discretion on the recipient's part is called for. However, the administration's scheme goes far beyond such correction. Fortunately, it is already being questioned and further adaptations will undoubtedly occur. In all, I find much to disagree with in the administration's vision of the role of the federal public sector and how it should be reduced, but its proposals have stimulated much interesting discussion. They may thus, after all, lead to an improved set of policies.

The Premises of the Administration's Approach

Beyond disagreement on particular points of policy, I am concerned with the ideological base of the administration's approach. The essence of the administration's outlook on economic policy is best summarized by the president's statement that "our problem will not be solved by government; the government is the problem." I think this is dead wrong. Of course the government poses problems, but so does the private sector. If these problems are to be solved, they are to be solved in unison. To think that a modern economy can exist without government's playing a significant role is to misread reality; and to base policy on that misreading is to invite disaster for a free society. Free markets, to be sure, are an ingredient of this society, but freedom means more than free markets. It involves deeper issues of human dignity and self-determination, and these go well beyond freedom to exchange. Freedom, as I read it, cannot be seen apart from the broader concept of a just society, and government is a necessary partner in securing it.

RESPONSES

William A. Niskanen: "Reducing the Federal Share of National Output"

One of the most important objectives of the Reagan administration is to reduce the federal government's share of national output. In 1980, total government outlays increased at about 17.5 percent; their growth in 1981 was reduced slightly to 14 percent and will prove to be about 11 percent in 1982. Unfortunately, although the rate of growth of outlays is slowing, the federal share of national output has gone up rather than down in the last two years, and is now something over 24 percent. So if we are to succeed in reducing the relative share of national output, either we have to maintain rather more severe budget discipline than has been the case to date or the economy must improve rather dramatically.

The fundamental political dilemma that we face is that Congress seems to want inconsistent things. That's not new, or maybe not surprising, but we face a situation in which Congress, for the most part, does not want to make the budget cuts the administration has recommended, does not really want to raise taxes, and does not want nor like the high deficits. And the problem both within the administration and in Congress will be to sort through alternatives, some of which many of us probably do not want, and to accept one in exchange for another.

The administration's FY 1983 budget, the first budget that we prepared from scratch, has roughly a 4 percent growth in nominal outlays. That puts us back on a meaningful path toward a reduced federal role in terms of total outlays in our economy. That budget will be the critical test as to whether Congress is prepared to support such a relatively reduced federal role.

The question of the deficit is torturous. I think one perspective that has not been widely understood is that the federal government, like all other institutions that were credit junkies during the 1970s, is having a very difficult time adjusting to lower inflation. That is true of all institutions that were betting on inflation and that looked good as long as inflation was higher than expected. The contrary occurs when inflation is coming down. The federal government faces a fiscal problem because the revenue effect of lower inflation is virtually immediate. Lower inflation lowers nominal revenues almost at once, but it reduces outlays, or outlay growth, only after a lag of about a year and a half, because of the lag between the base period in which cost-of-living adjustments (COLAs) are made and the period in which the additional payments under COLA arrangements are made. The consequence is that as long as inflation is declining, there will be a wedge between revenues and outlays. At some stage it will go away when the decline stops, but the wedge will look big for whatever period of time inflation does continue to fall. That number itself is on the order of several tens of billions of dollars for each one-point decline in inflation. So we find ourselves in a situation in which there does not seem to be any way to prevent the deficits from going up during a period of declining inflation, unless we are prepared either to intervene in cost-of-living indexing arrangements or to add a temporary tax.

There is also the question of what is an optimal distribution between tax and debt finance as a function of the composition of federal spending. The question of whether a major asset increase should be debt financed is basically a question of whether the right decision has been made. If the correct decision has been made, for example, to acquire tens of billions of dollars of military assets, then I see no reason why the federal government, unique among other institutions in American society, should not borrow to finance that capital acquisition. So the real question is whether the federal government is acquiring capital on net, and, second, whether the decision is correct—in other words, whether in future years this capital is going to be worth the taxes that must be paid during those years to finance the debt. In the event that the decision was correct on the capital acquisition, I see no reason for the federal government not to borrow to meet temporary capital acquisition surges in much the same way that any other institution does.

The fundamental issue of the deficit in my mind is the compact between the present and the future. I think all financial or fiduciary managers, including the fiscal managers of the federal government, have the responsibility to leave the fisc in as good or better shape when they leave as when they came. That involves questions, however, of what happens both on the asset side of the balance sheet and on the liability side.

Alice Rivlin: "The Deficit Dilemma"

We're not talking here just about Reaganomics; we're talking about a situation that faces the government as a result of actions that had very broad bipartisan and national support. I think just about everybody—and it was reflected in the votes in Congress—was agreed a year ago that we really needed to do four things at once. First, we needed to reduce the rate of growth of government spending, for various economic and noneconomic reasons—including the feelings that government had too heavy a hand in the economy, that incentives in many programs were negative. But at the same time we wanted to increase the real growth in defense. There was a consensus on both of those things, in the administration, on Capitol Hill, I think generally in the country. We also wanted to reduce the tax burden, not only because people don't like to pay taxes, but also because of the feeling that taxes, and corporate taxes particularly, were inhibiting in-

vestment and economic growth. Maybe we didn't solve the
problem very well, but there certainly was a general feeling
that depreciation allowances had been eroded by inflation,
that the marginal tax rates had crept up too high under the
influence of inflation over the years, and that something had
to be done about it. And everyone also agreed that it would be
a good thing to move towards a balanced budget.

Those are four things that, I think, everybody is still pretty
much agreed on. It's just that they're terribly hard to do. It
makes it easier if you have a very optimistic forecast about
economic growth; and the temptation to choose one existed
both in the administration and in Congress. Congress
chose—by voting on the administration's program—to accept a more optimistic set of assumptions than the mainstream of economic forecasters thought was likely. That is a
very tempting thing to do, because it makes the choices
somewhat easier. It has turned out that the mainstream economic forecasters were wrong in the short run. They were
too optimistic. And growth over the last year has been much
slower than most of us expected, in and out of the administration but especially within it. And we now start with a
recession-caused deficit and look ahead.

The scary thing is what happens if you look ahead. It is a
very different situation from what budgeteers have ever
faced before. All of us who have been around the budget
game for a long time got very used to the situation in which,
as you looked ahead, revenues rose faster than GNP while
outlays did not. As a result, wherever you started from, even
if it was a large recession-caused deficit, the deficit came
down in your projection. It didn't always come down in real
life, because policies changed, but a current policy forecast
meant a smaller deficit. That is no longer true. And it doesn't
really matter whose forecast you're using—whether you're
using the administration's, which is still, I think, on the optimistic side of the pack of forecasters, or that of the Congressional Budget Office, which is roughly in the middle—if

you look forward with a positive rate of growth, but not an extraordinarily high one, you see the same picture. Because of the tax cut last year—which was designed exactly to do this—the rate of growth of revenues is considerably slower than the rate of growth of GNP, and outlays grow at about the same rate as GNP, with the domestic side coming down in compensation for the defense increase. There is a shift of resources from domestic to defense—it's not huge in the complex of such things, but it's substantial—yet the real problem is that these things compensate for each other: roughly speaking, in the absence of a policy change, outlays stay at about 23 percent of GNP. The revenues will come down from about 21 percent to about 18, which means the deficit will escalate from around 2 percent to around 5 percent of GNP. That is large by anybody's calculation. You can reestimate, you can talk about deficits relative to this or that, but you are still talking about a very large deficit and it doesn't go away in the minds of Congress or the financial community. We have this enormous problem that, if policy is not changed, we will be financing a very, very large government deficit relative to anything, and this is very likely to put increased upward pressure on interest rates, as the Federal Reserve has told us. That is the current dilemma.

David Berson: "Will Tax Incentives Increase Investment?"

An increase in investment expenditures on equipment and structures by business is the means by which many analysts believe that the *long-run* economic goals of lower inflation and higher labor productivity growth can be achieved. Many economists argue that a significant part of the poor performance of labor productivity since the mid-1970s is directly due to a slowdown in capital formation.

Reversal of this slowdown will require large increases in the share of GNP going to business investment. In 1981, the outgoing Council of Economic Advisers estimated that the real investment share would have to increase substantially to the 12.5 to 13 percent range in order to meet this need. Historically, this share has averaged about 10 percent.

The Reagan administration has proposed the Accelerated Cost Recovery System (ACRS) as the primary means for increasing investment. There are two questions that we can look at concerning this proposal. First, how strong will the effects be on increasing investment? And second, is it the best method for accomplishing this increase? The Economic Recovery Tax Act (ERTA) of 1981 included the ACRS as its most important element on the business side. But there were three other components to the act. First was the introduction of leasing rules. Second was an increase in the investment tax credit for some types of equipment. Finally, small business was allowed to expense up to $5,000 of new investment in 1982, rising to $10,000 in 1985 and thereafter. The Tax Equity and Fiscal Responsibility Act of 1982 made some substantial changes in the 1981 ERTA for business. Most of these changes did not affect the ACRS, however, and those that did were relatively minor. For example, the act repealed the further acceleration of ACRS personal property rates that were to be applied to property placed in service after 1984.

I have looked at implementation of the ACRS in three different models of investment behavior: a cash-flow with accelerator term model (CFA), a Jorgenson-type neoclassical model (N), and the investment equations from the Data Resources, Incorporated macroeconomic model (DRI). The calculations are based on the assumption that budget deficits are held constant so that crowding-out effects do not occur; that is, that real interest rates are held constant. The figures in the table are estimated investment/GNP ratios.

	1981–85 avg.	1986–89 avg.	1981–89 avg.
CFA	10.6%	11.3%	10.9%
N	11.7	12.6	12.1
DRI	10.8	11.8	11.2

These results suggest that investment will be substantially stimulated, but that it will quite likely not be enough to bring the ratio to the 12.5 to 13 percent level. The average of all three models for the last half of the decade is about 12 percent, and for the entire decade is about 11.5 percent.

The second point is whether or not the ACRS is the *best* means to increase investment. The 1982 *Economic Report* states, "The ACRS does not treat all types of business investment equally. Although favorable to all new investment, ACRS is relatively more favorable to investment in equipment." Given the large shift in investment towards equipment and away from structures that has occurred over the last twenty years, it is probably not desirable on efficiency grounds to implement a tax change that is obviously nonneutral in this manner. I have also looked at the likely effects of an alternative tax cut on investment: an increase in the investment tax credit (ITC). This too is a nonneutral tax cut with respect to the demand for different types of capital—but it is much easier to create a neutral ITC than a neutral accelerated depreciation. Based on the criterion of "most bang for the buck" (additional amounts of investment per dollar of tax revenue loss), the clear winner is the ITC.

	Tax cut	1981–85 avg.	1981–89 avg.
CFA	ITC	.24	.46
	ACRS	.19	.37
N	ITC	1.22	1.14
	ACRS	.79	.56
DRI	ITC	1.16	1.15
	ACRS	.57	.56

V

Further Aspects of the Reagan Program

7

Wm. CRAIG STUBBLEBINE

The Economics of the New Federalism

The New Federalism is the one major component of the administration's overall program that has failed thus far to gain adoption in any form. A midterm report on the New Federalism therefore must focus on proposals rather than on policies in execution. Nonetheless, since the administration is pressing forward and since the governors continue to debate, it is worth asking what economic theory can tell us, briefly, about the merits and demerits of the president's proposals as presently constituted.

We should begin by summarizing what the administration has proposed so far. In original form, the administration's plan included the following:

- Assumption by the federal government of full financial and administrative responsibility for Medicaid (currently shared with the states on a matching basis ranging from 50 to 77 percent), while continuing its responsibility for Medicare.

- Assumption by state governments of the full cost of food stamps (currently federally funded and state administered) and of Aid to Families with Dependent Children (currently shared with the states on a matching basis ranging from 50 to 77 percent).

- "Turn-back" to the state and local governments of various federal programs in education and training, social services, transportation, community development, and revenue sharing.

- Consolidation of various federal categorical grant programs into block grants for child welfare, rental rehabilitation, training and employment, welfare administration, vocational and adult education, education for the handicapped, and rehabilitation services.

- Creation of a federal "trust fund" financed by existing federal excise taxes and the windfall profits tax on oil, on which the states may draw to find substitutes for the "turn-back" programs. Over time, the federal taxes financing the trust fund would be eliminated, leaving the states to enact replacement levies should they so decide.

In response to reactions from various constituencies, the administration offered to revise its proposals in the following respects:

- Food stamps would be retained at the federal level.

- Medicaid would be "broken apart," with federal responsibility limited to "basic coverage" and the states sharing fiscal responsibility with the federal government for "long-term care" and "optional services."

• Some general federal revenues would be allocated to supporting the "turn-back trust fund."

The literature of economics provides two approaches that can be brought to bear on the problem of federalism— classical theory and public choice theory. Each sheds light on a different aspect of the phenomenon.

Classical Theory

In his definitive treatment of the classical theory of federalism, Wallace Oates notes that

from an economic standpoint, the obvious attraction of the federal form of government is that it combines the strengths of unitary government with those of decentralization. Each level of government, rather than attempting to perform all the functions of the public sector, does what it can do best. The central government presumably accepts primary responsibility for stabilizing the economy, for achieving the most equitable distribution of income, and for providing certain public goods that influence significantly the welfare of all members of society. Complementing these operations, subcentral governments can supply those public goods and services that are of primary interest only to the residents of their respective jurisdictions. In this way, a federal form of government offers the best promise of a successful resolution of the problems that constitute the economic *raison d'etre* of the public sector. It is in this sense that federalism may, in economic terms, be described as the optimal form of government.[1]

Behind this outlook are two concepts familiar to economists: "economies of scale" and "externalities." Economies of scale exist when a producer of a good or service experiences decreasing average costs per unit of output as the quantity of output increases. If, beyond some level of output, average costs of production begin to increase, it can be argued that the production is optimally distributed among producers if each operates at an output level corresponding to minimum average cost.

Applying this principle, one can argue that production of a collective good or service optimally should take place at the

level of government that is in the best position to minimize
the average cost per unit of production. For example, having
each of two communities served by its own television relay
tower may be a more costly way of producing television
reception than using a single tower of height sufficient to
serve both communities. In such a case, the good would be
supplied best by a unit of government that spanned the land
area of the two communities. There are other cases in which,
from this standpoint, two or more levels of government
would be optimal.

Externalities arise when the goods or services produced, or
not produced, by one community have repercussions for the
welfare of others. For example, assume two communities occupy the same air basin under conditions wherein the quality
of the air is uniform throughout the basin. Residents in both
communities engage in activities that throw pollutants into
the air: driving, burning trash, heating homes, operating industrial plants, etc. Reducing the level of pollution means
some or all residents must bear costs—through higher taxes,
higher prices for goods and services consumed, or lower incomes from employment and investment in the area.

Although all residents have an interest in pollution abate-
ment, a resident of either community may perceive that controls on pollutants by his community will have little impact
on the quality of the air he breathes. The residents of each
community are likely to perceive that their interests would
be best served if the *other* community would adopt stringent
controls over polluting activities. Each community, therefore, is led to oppose local controls and to advocate controls
for neighboring communities.

By contrast, a more inclusive unit of government may
secure the support of the residents of the two communities.
In effect, the more inclusive unit of government provides an
arena in which the externality is internalized. At the same
time, each community may be the most viable organizing en-
tity for those goods and services for which spillovers to other

communities are nonexistent or nil. In the latter case, two or more levels of government would be optimal from an externality standpoint.

There is a difference between an "economies of scale" justification for federalism and an "externality" justification. In the first, what is passed to a more inclusive unit of government is responsibility for production; responsibility for the *funding* of production may be located at any level of government, even the lowest. In the second, what is passed to the more inclusive unit of government is responsibility for coordination or joint decision making of the activity, not its production per se. In the nature of things, externality issues are likely to be centered on distributing the burden of activities undertaken by the government unit and, consequently, on the quantity of the activity at issue.

Taken together, the two concepts provide support for the idea of a multiplicity of fiscal jurisdictions:

The optimal form of federal government to provide the set of *n* public goods would be one in which there exists a level of government for each subset of the population over which the consumption of a public good is defined.[2]

Unless the subsets are few, this optimal form may imply a complex layering of fiscal jurisdictions. In the context of American federalism, the Constitution recognizes only two levels: the federal government and the governments of the several states. By contrast, state constitutions may recognize various governmental units covering the spectrum from counties, cities, townships, school districts, to a variety of special districts—all of which may have responsibility for various collective activities.

Whether the present layering is optimal from the classical standpoint may be a matter of some speculation. Sheer practicality of political decision making will impose some restraint on the proliferation of jurisdictions. At the same time, an extraordinary degree of complexity can be found. For example, Orange County (California), with a population of two million in 785 square miles, is reputed to have some 14,000 separate property taxing areas produced by one county government, 26 city governments, 35 school districts, and 151 special districts.

Public Choice Analysis

In contrast to the classical approach, public choice theory stresses that voter-taxpayer-beneficiaries will face differing costs of acquiring additional units of collective goods and services depending upon the fiscal jurisdiction to which responsibility for funding and production is assigned. Voters have an incentive to assign responsibility to the public sector only if it promises to be a lower cost supplier than the private sector and, within the public sector, to assign responsibility to the jurisdiction that promises the lowest tax price.

Contrasting private sector "market prices" and public sector "tax prices" helps to clarify the difference between private and public sector funding. In the private sector, competition among firms for customers and resources tends to produce equality between resource cost and private purchase price. At the same time, independent adjustment leads customers to extend the quantities they purchase up to the point where the (marginal) valuation they place on the activity equals the price charged by the firm. Thus, in private equilibrium, the resource costs of services provided tends to equal the prices paid for those services, and both equal the valuations placed upon the services by the purchaser-beneficiary.

By contrast, in the public sector, the tax law and benefit allocation rules sever the link between resource costs and tax prices faced by the body politic. Majority voting, in turn, severs the link between tax prices and voter-taxpayer-beneficiary valuations. In consequence, the existence of a public sector will inevitably result in (some) services being provided at tax prices in excess of valuation and (some) services being provided at tax prices less than valuation. Members of the body politic whose valuations are less than resource costs, but greater than the tax prices they face, will be led to seek and to approve extensions in the quantities of collective goods and services they would classify as "efficient" if required to bear the resource costs of the extensions. Others whose valuations are greater than resource costs, but less than the tax prices they face, will be led to oppose extensions of the public sector they would classify as "efficient" if only they could face the resource costs of the extensions.

In a world of multiple fiscal jurisdictions, four implications follow from the tax-price analysis. First, individual members of the national body politic have an incentive to search among fiscal jurisdictions—the county, the state, and the national level—while assigning use or allocative responsibility to the least inclusive jurisdiction. That federal grant-in-aid programs should be sought by, and their prospective denial or withdrawal condemned by, local government officials should come as no surprise. Third, with majority voting, no local fiscal jurisdiction can secure favorable action on its own proposals for central jurisdiction without the support of other localities. The coalition-building process naturally tends to an overexpansion of funding by more inclusive jurisdictions. Fourth, funding and production responsibilities may be assigned to more inclusive jurisdictions without regard either to economies of scale or to externality considerations, since members of the coalition majority seek to maximize their own welfare and not the welfare of the whole.

Theoretical Merits of the Reagan Proposals

Classical theory suggests that responsibility for redistribution of income should be located at the most inclusive level of government. To the extent that the president's New Federalism would increase federal emphasis on income security, including health services, it corresponds well with theory.

At the same time, the president's proposal to shift fiscal responsibility for Aid to Families with Dependent Children to the states runs counter to both classical and public choice theory. Indeed, theory would suggest that pressures to redistribute income, resulting from either or both the externality of caring about the poor wherever they may reside and the tax price incentives to shift funding to the most inclusive fiscal jurisdiction, could be accommodated most effectively by some version of the "negative income tax." In such schemes, the federal government would disperse funds to, rather than collect taxes from, those below the national poverty level after allowance for dependents, medical expenses, and other deductions and credits. At the national level, the tax price of income redistribution would be manifest while the fiscal competition inherent in less inclusive jurisdictional funding responsibility would be obviated.

To strip the federal budget, as the administration proposes to do, of programs augmenting the supply of collective goods and services other than redistribution would seem consistent with classical theory, but it runs counter to public choice analysis. It may be tempting to explain the expanded federal role in the funding of collective goods since the turn of the century as a response to the increasing interdependence, or externality, of a mobile, mass communication society. There is, however, little or no evidence that the accommodation provided by state and local governments in the absence of federal funding would leave unexploited significant economies of scale or externality. That is, the quantities of collective goods and services that the residents of less inclusive communities would seek to provide for themselves are likely to be at least equal to the quantities that would satisfy those who reside outside the community.

While seeking to deny the tax-price incentives at the federal level, the president's New Federalism proposals would do nothing to restructure the institutional arrangements within which they arise. Even were they to be enacted into law, their preservation through time would require a new attitude toward the proper role of the federal government—one that goes beyond espousing "government closest to the people." Central to such an attitude would be a distinction between properly federal activities and commonly shared concerns. The two principal examples of properly federal activities are national defense and the conduct of international relations. The federal coordination critical to their success implies that federal financing in such cases is both required and appropriate.

Commonly shared concerns, on the other hand, include activities where success or failure of the response in one community would have little or no impact on the prospects for success or failure in any other community. For example, every school district in the nation has had and will have students who would rather play than study. Assigning fiscal responsibility for truant officers to the federal government would relieve individual school districts of a portion of their fiscal responsibility. It would not offer, however, any more effective response to truancy than would a program funded wholly by each school district. The burden of higher taxes for federally funded truant officers in every school district would be felt throughout the United States—as would local funding of truant officers. What would be different under federal funding would be the distribution of the tax burden.

A sound fiscal federalism would fund federal programs at the federal level and leave the funding of responses to commonly shared concerns to state and local governments.

RESPONSE

Wallace E. Oates: "Strengths and Weaknesses of the New Federalism"

As Craig mentioned, the basic, professed objective of the Reagan administration's New Federalism is a clarification of the division of functions between the federal government and the states and localities. While the objective is surely laudable in principle, I think all of us, including the administration, recognize that there exists no neat, well-defined separation of roles.

The fact seems to be that the responsibility for functions inevitably cuts across levels of government. Nevertheless, there are some useful distinctions concerning the appropriate roles for different levels of government. Although they don't produce a fully well-defined set of roles for each level of government, they do provide some insights and some useful guidelines.

The textbooks frequently define the basic roles of the public sector as consisting of three distinct functions: first, a macroeconomic stabilization role, consisting of the use of monetary and fiscal policies to regulate levels of employment and the price level; second, a redistributive role, with a particular emphasis on financial assistance for the poor; and third, an allocation role involving the provision of goods and services that, for various reasons, are not forthcoming in appropriate levels through the operation of the private sector of the economy.

I think there is general agreement on the proposition that the macroeconomic stabilization role, however it is to be pursued, really must remain a responsibility of the central government.

If we look at the redistributive function, and particularly at providing assistance for the poor, there is again a case—

although perhaps not as strong as the macroeconomic
case—for central government leadership and responsibility.
Decentralized governments face serious constraints in their
ability to provide support for low-income households. There
is a long history of economic analysis of this issue. A locality,
for example, that attempts to undertake a generous program
to provide for the poor is likely to find itself attracting low-
income households and driving out higher-income units as a
result of the higher tax rates needed to finance the program.

Finally, as regards allocation (the provision of various
goods and services), the central government obviously has a
role in providing for those services such as national defense
and foreign policy that affect the welfare of the whole country. State and local governments come into play in providing
those services that are of primary interest to residents of
their respective jurisdictions—local roads and schools, and
so forth.

If one takes this perspective on federal finance and applies
it to the proposals that make up the package under the New
Federalism, one very disturbing element sticks out: the
proposal to return the financing of AFDC and the food
stamp programs to state and local governments. This proposal turns the division of functions that I've talked about
topsy-turvy. In fact, President Reagan has said, "Financial
assistance to the poor is a legitimate responsibility of states
and localities."

In this particular regard, it seems to me that the New
Federalism is based on a misunderstanding of the appropriate roles of government in a federal system. I really can't see
any compelling economic rationale for the swap of AFDC and
food stamp programs for Medicaid. The inevitable result is
some future decline in assistance for the poor, because states
and localities will not maintain these transfer programs at
present levels.

A related objective of the New Federalism is an explicit
and heavy emphasis on devolution, a return to the states and

localities of responsibilities that, in the administration's view, have been improperly assumed by the federal government. And the approach here involves basic reform of the intergovernmental system of grants: first, an elimination of many categorical grant-in-aid programs through consolidation into large block grants; and second, a reduction in grants with a return of responsibilities to the state and local governments accompanied by a turning back of some sources of revenues.

Intergovernmental grants, here and in other federal countries as well, have become a widely used policy instrument. Federal governments have found them a very flexible fiscal tool that can be used to provide inducements for decentralized levels of government to respond appropriately where there are externalities or where the national interest is at stake, without the federal government's actually assuming full responsibility for the role. From an economic perspective, intergovernmental grants are typically seen as serving three different objectives. The first has to do with external effects, providing inducements such as matching grants for state and local governments to undertake or extend programs where there is a clear national interest at stake. Second, there is the role of providing relatively low-income jurisdictions with the ability to offer satisfactory levels of key public services while maintaining tax rates roughly equivalent to those elsewhere. Third, perhaps, is a revenue-sharing function, which essentially amounts to a substitution of part of the federal tax system for state and local taxes without assuming directly the expenditure role. By substituting part of the federal tax system for part of the state and local tax systems, one ends up with an overall tax structure that is, in some sense perhaps, more desirable in terms of its incidence, its pattern of payments, and also its effects on the operation of the market system. For this third function, we are not trying to get state and local governments to provide specific services, so unconditional or "lump sum grants," as they are called, are appropriate.

Now, if we look at the Reagan program in this setting, we find the consolidation of many specific purpose grants into large block grants. I think this is in part a response to the rapid proliferation of categorical grants into many hundreds of distinct grant programs over the past decade or two. One can certainly make a compelling case for consolidation, if just on the grounds of eliminating overlap and providing simplification. We should, however, evaluate these categorical grants on a program-by-program basis to see if there is some compelling national interest that would suggest some kind of federal intervention. My sense is that, certainly, a number of these grant programs would not pass this test.

More generally, a movement to broad block grants will certainly provide less stimulus to state and local spending than will the categorical grants that they are displacing. These are fungible funds. State and local governments can use dollars under block grants simply to replace funds that they would have spent otherwise, and effectively use these dollars for state and local tax relief.

A move to broad block grants, then, will provide less stimulus to the state and local sector. But the Reagan program aims ultimately at a gradual cessation of these programs. Many of these block grants are transitory in character, and the turn-back proposal will involve eventually eliminating a lot of these programs and turning the sources of funding back to the states. Now the Reagan administration is interested, at least as I read it, in reducing the size of the government sector, perhaps at the state-local level as well as the federal level. An interesting question is whether or not these programs for reform of the intergovernmental grant system will lead to this end. Suppose, for example, that a central government were to come into a local jurisdiction, collect a hundred dollars per capita in the form of a federal tax, and then turn right around and hand that hundred dollars per capita back to the jurisdiction, not to the individuals but rather to the local government in the jurisdiction. What is the likely impact of this transaction on levels of local government spending in that jurisdiction?

The so-called "veil hypothesis" in economics suggests that for a wide variety of budget decisions this will have basically no effect at all. What will happen is that the local government will simply take the receipts it gets from the central government, substitute those for taxes that it would have collected otherwise from its residents, and end up with an unchanged level and pattern of budgetary activity. So this kind of transaction would appear to be a relatively neutral one. If we turn it around, then, the Reagan administration, in taking away grants but giving back the revenues at the same time through a tax cut, is effectively having a roughly neutral effect on the size of the public sector.

However, there's a large body of other work in economics on this issue that is more empirical in character and suggests that the veil hypothesis doesn't stand up very well; that, in fact, if you look at actual budgetary behavior, you find that the propensity of local governments to spend out of lump sum grants is a good deal higher than the propensity of local governments to spend out of an increase in private income in their jurisdictions.

Now, if this is the case (and the empirical work makes a pretty good case for this result), then the net effect of a reduction in grant programs, while at the same time cutting down on federal tax revenues, will indeed be to reduce the level of spending at state and local levels.

8

THOMAS GALE MOORE

The Reagan Deregulation Program: An Assessment

For those who believe that government policy should be directed toward increasing economic competition in order to benefit consumers, the effects of the Reagan administration's regulatory policy have been mixed. The good news from the standpoint of overall economic efficiency is that the Department of Justice dismissed the IBM case and the Federal Trade Commission dismissed its ten-year-old antitrust case against the three major cereal-makers; oil prices were decontrolled; and auto passive restraint requirements were lifted. Most notably, the president issued an executive

order requiring that all major regulatory actions by administration agencies be subject to cost-benefit analysis. The bad
news is that there has been a substantial retreat from competitive market principles in transportation, a jettisoning of
market approaches to environmental regulation, and failures by the administration to set forth significant reforms in
the Clean Air Act and to propose the deregulation of natural
gas. For broadcasting regulation, the record is mixed; no
progress has been made in deregulating financial institutions; and, outside of an aborted attempt to abolish the Consumer Product Safety Commission, there has been no change
in the field of consumer product regulation.

Cost-Benefit Analysis

The administration takes the greatest pride in Executive
Order 12291, which requires that all executive branch agencies subject any new regulations to a cost-benefit analysis.
The order also gives the Office of Management and Budget
(OMB) oversight authority over this process and requires
that agencies establish a schedule for the review of all existing regulations to determine whether they meet the cost-
benefit test.

The administration claims that the rate of introduction of
new regulations has been sharply reduced, pointing to a major decline in the number of pages in the Federal Register as
evidence. Moreover, it seems clear that a significant number
of the "midnight" regulations issued at the last moment by
the Carter administration have been forestalled. In many
cases their implementation has been simply postponed; in
others the regulations have been abolished or changed substantially. Unfortunately, there appears to be little progress
in the repeal of existing rules that do not meet the cost-
benefit test.

Yet how effective that test will be in practice is an open
question. While cost-benefit analysis has the advantage of

focusing discussion on the relevant issues, the actual outcome often may depend on the ideological predilection of the analyst. For example, W. Kip Viscusi, director of Duke University's Center for the Study of Business Regulation, has criticized the National Highway Traffic Safety Administration for rolling back its passive restraint standard on the grounds that one investigation has shown the benefits of airbags to exceed the costs.[1]

The problems of cost-benefit analysis are illustrated by recent controversy over the proposed Occupational Safety and Health Administration (OSHA) rule on chemical labeling. This is the first major rule proposed by the Reagan administration that would be very costly to industry. It would require manufacturers to label hazardous chemicals in the workplace. OSHA estimated the benefits at $5.2 billion (present value) and the costs at $2.6 billion—clearly a winner. However, OMB sharply criticized OSHA's approach and found that the benefits were only a meager $65 million. To settle the issue, the Presidential Task Force on Regulatory Relief commissioned an independent study by W. Kip Viscusi, who found, using an entirely different methodology, that the benefits were only $2.8 billion—which, however, is still greater than the costs. In part because the Chemical Manufacturers Association and the American Petroleum Institute have favored much of the proposed standard, Vice-President Bush decided to override OMB and publish the rule. It will still have to be submitted to OMB before it becomes final.[2]

This case raises several disturbing issues. Obviously, if two government bureaus in the same administration can produce benefit figures that differ by 8,000 percent (with an independent estimate arriving at a third divergent figure), then the precision of cost-benefit analysis leaves something to be desired. If such a spread is common, cost-benefit analysis can presumably be used to justify or to block practically any regulation.

OSHA's defense of the proposed regulation on the grounds that industry supported it is also disturbing. As OMB argued, most of the major firms are already labeling, so the greatest impact would be on the smaller companies. The American Petroleum Institute has argued specifically that the larger petroleum companies have self-imposed labeling requirements while many of the smaller do not. Thus the proposal could actually reduce competition.

Bias toward Big Business

This case illustrates what appears to be a disturbing trend in the Reagan administration: a bias towards benefiting business, especially big business. Perhaps this is desirable. Past administrations have had an anti—big business bias, and some support for our major corporations may be warranted. Certainly one of the greatest successes in the administration has been the dismissal of the IBM case, which, as antitrust chief William Baxter found, was without merit. The dropping of the cereal case also was overdue. But the government's approach to the regulation of specific industries shows a bias toward benefiting the industry rather than fostering competition.

The actions of the Federal Communications Commission (FCC), under the leadership of its new chairman Mark Fowler, demonstrate the ambiguities in the administration's position. Mr. Fowler replaced Charles Ferris, whom Carter appointed as chairman of the FCC and who guided the commission in reducing economic regulation. Mr. Fowler was a broadcast lobbyist who represented the Virginia Association of Broadcasters; his firm's clients include many broadcast and private radio licensees. *Broadcasting* magazine, which represents the industry, welcomed his selection. *The Wall Street Journal* quoted the new chairman as stating, shortly before he took office, "If introducing 30 more radio stations into a particular market erodes the broadcasters' economic base so they can't afford to produce news and public affairs shows anymore, is that in the public interest? In some places, it's hard for broadcasters to do well. It's been very tough to survive, you know, because there are already too many of them."[3] Such statements suggest a total absence of understanding of the competitive process and the benefits of competition.

About two years ago the FCC unanimously endorsed the concept of shrinking channel spacing in order to permit more stations. The National Association of Broadcasters, the industry's lobbying organization, bitterly opposed the plan, which would have made channel spacing in the Western Hemisphere consistent with that in the rest of the world. After the plan's approval, three commissioners who strongly supported it left the FCC, and with these commissioners gone, Fowler led the FCC to a four-to-two vote to reverse the decision. The broadcast industry is quite happy with this change but, in the absence of more competition, the public is the loser. Some have estimated that, had deregulation continued, as many as 1,400 new stations would have been possible.

On the other hand, Mr. Fowler has advocated the elimination of the Fairness Doctrine and has urged Congress to repeal the equal time requirements for political candidates. He claims to be in favor of competition and has no intention of protecting existing broadcasters. Nevertheless, he has expressed some reservations about a proposal to permit more VHF television stations. So far, the commission has moved ahead with its plan to permit new low-powered TV stations. It is also considering increasing the number of orbital slots for communications satellites, which would increase the competition among communications common carriers. The FCC also has proposed the elimination of all present restrictions on subscription TV so that it can compete better with cable.

In a number of other regulatory sectors there has been no progress whatsoever. For example, the Depository Institutions Deregulatory Committee has twice refused to approve modest increases in the interest rates that banks and savings and loans can pay their depositors. The administration did attempt to abolish the Consumer Product Safety Commission, but Congress would not approve. There has been no appreciable change at the Nuclear Regulatory Commission, although candidate Reagan strongly supported improving the regulatory environment for nuclear power during his presidential campaign. There has also been no visible change at the Securities Exchange Commission.

Natural Gas and Environmental Regulation

However, the Reagan administration's greatest failures probably lie in its inability or unwillingness to propose changes in either the regulation of natural gas or environmental controls. The current natural gas regulatory morass is extremely costly to the economy and undermines its self-sufficiency. At present, natural gas from certain very costly sources, such as deep wells, is uncontrolled and sells for about $9 per million BTUs (British thermal units) at the wellhead, while in some cases controlled gas sells for less than $1. For purposes of establishing consumer prices, expensive gas is presently averaged in with cheap gas, with the result that waste is encouraged. Gas pipelines import the fuel from Mexico and Canada at well above average wellhead prices, contributing not only to waste but also to our dependence on others for essential fuels. A sensible strategy would be to speed up decontrol and extend it to all forms of natural gas. This might result in a price jump of about 40 percent at the wellhead and 20 percent at the retail level. No doubt such a move would have adverse political consequences, but the improvement in our economy would be significant.

The other great failure of omission is the inability of the administration to propose and support changes in the Clean Air Act. Robert Crandall of the Brookings Institution has recommended that auto emission standards be partially rolled back, that the requirement to install scrubbers on all new coal-fired boilers be scrapped, that the uniform air pollution control technology for new facilities be modified, and that a cost-benefit analysis be used in establishing ambient air quality standards.[4] Early in the administration, the Council of Economic Advisers also suggested some revisions, but the suggestions were rejected by Environmental Protection Agency (EPA) director Anne Gorsuch. Unfortunately, the current approach to deregulation at the EPA appears to be one of cutting the budget and staff of the agency while leaving the rules and legislation intact. Such a strategy ignores the fact that much of the harm stemming from environmental regulation is a product of written legislation rather than zealous bureaucrats. Without a change in the law, little progress can be expected. Even though economic incentives could cut in half the cost of environmental regulation while reducing pollution, Ms. Gorsuch has opposed their introduction. Several key aides who supported such approaches have resigned or been forced out.

Failures in Transportation

The worst performance of the Reagan administration lies in the regulation of transportation. Judging by the standard that policy should be directed toward promoting competition, governmental actions have been perverse for airline regulation, maritime policy, and Interstate Commerce Commission (ICC) performance. Under the Carter administration, the Civil Aeronautics Board (CAB) had proposed restrictions on the antitrust immunity of airlines participating in the international aviation cartel IATA. Early in the Reagan administration's term, the CAB announced that it would lift antitrust immunity for rate making on the North Atlantic run. Faced with protests from foreign governments, the president asked the CAB to postpone its order. Subsequently, the administration has worked out with the CAB, and supposedly also with European governments, an agreement to permit participation in IATA rate making in return for authorizing a range in which carriers could freely price. The proposed bottom of the range is above the lowest rates currently charged, so the impact will be to eliminate the lowest fares. While it may be premature to panic, there is growing pressure to bring back some airline regulation.

Recently the administration proposed legislation to Congress that would exempt from the antitrust laws agreements by the maritime industry on rates, profit sharing, cargo sharing, and capacity limitations. This is clearly anticompetitive. It also will not benefit the American merchant marine, which is saddled with much higher costs than foreign carriers due to restrictive government requirements. By requesting such legislation, the Reagan administration has again shown a lack of concern for promoting competition.

The administration has made its policy quite clear on the regulation of surface freight transportation. Immediately upon taking office it asked Darius Gaskins, the deregulation-minded chairman, to resign. In his place was appointed Reese H. Taylor, a lawyer who had formerly chaired the Nevada Public Utilities Commission and who had represented the Arizona Motor Tariff Bureau. According to the *New York Times,* Mr. Taylor was suggested by the Teamsters Union.[5] Since his appointment, the ICC has construed the Motor Carrier Act of 1980 in the most restrictive way. Applicants for general commodity certificates are being denied because they cannot show that they have shippers who want to use their services for all possible commodities. Requests for authority to serve wide territories have been restricted to particular cities, although such restrictions appear to be inconsistent with the spirit of the Motor Carrier Act. And the commission has limited certificates to only the commodities listed in the application.

For example, Hagen, Inc., a Sioux City, Iowa, trucking

firm, applied for authority to haul general commodities nationwide. It asserted that a fifty-state grant would allow it to consolidate its operations, which were restricted by numerous and fragmented local authorities. In September the ICC review board granted authority only for "transporting essentially the traffic of those shippers at the points or facilities where shippers demonstrate a need for service." In part, Hagen was restricted to hauling chemicals between Terra Chemicals International, Inc., with locations in seventeen states, and other points in the U.S. Other similarly limited authority was granted to Hagen.[6] The board's actions fell far short of the fifty-state grant that would have increased the efficiency of the Hagen system.

Mr. Taylor has taken a narrow view of price competition. When carriers have negotiated lower rates with individual shippers, Taylor has called the rates "discriminatory" and "illegal." In a recent case, Roadway Express was entering a new market and, as firms often do in that type of situation, it offered a low introductory rate as a promotional gimmick. Mr. Taylor said this looked discriminatory and voted to suspend the rate while it was being investigated.

Recently, Mr. Taylor has been claiming to be in favor of deregulation and is arguing that his actions are only carrying out the law. The ICC has sent a bill to Congress to abolish the needs test for the granting of new certificates. In his letter accompanying the bill, Mr. Taylor concluded that "an entry standard, based on public need, is no longer useful." However, he also wants more stringent fitness criteria that include "financial fitness, operational fitness and safety fitness." Mr. Taylor's letter went on to say, "More specifically, with respect to financial fitness, an applicant would only need to describe its present or future financial capability to provide the proposed service. In evaluating financial fitness, the Commission would consider the problems that can be caused to the shipping public through the cessation of operations by a carrier. . . . We would envision that operational fitness would encompass the applicant's plans, knowledge, or experience to conduct the proposed service. With respect to operational fitness, the Commission's concern should be whether the applicant will be capable of performing the service within a reasonable period of time without undue risk to the public."[7] Even though Mr. Taylor claims that these standards are not intended to restrict entry, they clearly could have that effect.

While Mr. Taylor may have become a deregulator, he has resisted the idea of simply eliminating all entry controls. When the proposed new entry standard was sent to Congress, ICC commissioner Robert C. Gresham wrote that "unless this proposal is revised substantially, it easily could be used to retreat to the less competitive oriented regulatory environment which predated the Motor Carrier Act of 1980 and lead to a greater degree of regulatory control over the motor carrier industry."[8]

In summary, the behavior of this administration suggests that to Republicans deregulation means reducing the cost of regulation to industry, no doubt a worthy goal. However, regulation that increases prices by reducing competition also aids industry and is therefore welcome. Increasing the profits of the trucking industry by restricting competition is not the same thing as promoting free enterprise. It is unfortunate that the current administration has failed to match its free-market rhetoric with free-market policies.

RESPONSES

Ross D. Eckert: "Regulation and Self-Interest"

I have no major disagreement with Professor Moore's fine paper. What interests me most about this whole affair is why different administrations seem to choose regulatory policies with different emphases. We were all probably just as surprised that the Reagan administration has ignored certain policies and portions of deregulation that we thought to be part of its program as we were surprised at some of the Carter administration's actions. The question is why this has occurred. Since I am an economist, I will confine my remarks strictly to political science. It is important to start with first principles. The major political parties are structured very similarly on the issue of regulation or deregulation. Each has similar problems to overcome in formulating policy on this matter. Each of the two parties has essentially two wings out of which to form some consensus. I call these wings the reformers and the axgrinders.

Among the Republicans, of course, or the people who are identified with them, there are such people as are now prominent in the administration—James C. Miller, William Baxter, William Niskanen, and Murray Weidenbaum. In the case of Democrats, or the people who are identified with them, there have been Alfred Kahn, Elizabeth Bailey, Michael Levine, Darius Gaskins, and George Eads. These are all either economists or lawyers with strong interest in economic matters, and on these issues they espouse positions that are not very different. On most of the regulation or deregulation issues you could take any of these people, reverse them with those who work for the other party, and end up with little difference on the particular issue.

The axgrinders, of course, tend to ignore basic economic principles and to look out for their own interests. In the case of Democrats, the axgrinders take the form chiefly of the "public interest lawyers" and like-minded followers who benefit from regulation. Their actions increase the demand for the services of lawyers, from whose ranks they are largely drawn. They consist mainly of people who intend to make their careers either in government or in public interest lobbies. The Republican axgrinders also benefit from regulation. They are often protectionist or mercantilist types who live off the government in much the same way that the public interest lawyers do, except that this group lives more in the private sector and the other group more in the public sector. Neither group is very adept at distinguishing between private enterprise and free enterprise.

Now, which of these two wings dominates the regulatory policies of the party in power? The competition for influence depends on complexities that I am not competent to judge. But in the Reagan administration it was clear very early on as to what the nature of the competition would be and, in large measure, how it would turn out. Ronald Reagan, along with Edward Kennedy, was one of the early prominent political figures in this country to have embraced deregulation, but it is ironic that actual policies of Reagan's administration to date often have embraced other goals.

The large number of scholarly studies that have been written mainly by economists but to some extent by attorneys suggest that outcomes of regulation are often contrary to statutory intention and produce more costs than benefits. These apply to freight, passengers, communication, environment, and health and safety. To the reformers of either party, deregulation means deregulating all of those areas and searching for rules that have more benefits than costs rather than the other way around. As that gets translated through the political system, of course, the reformers' policy does not necessarily dominate. In the Carter administration, deregulation clearly meant freight, passengers, and communications but not automobile hardware, OSHA (Occupational Safety and Health Administration), or the EPA (Environmental Protection Agency). In the Reagan administration, it has been largely the reverse. Political accommodations are complex and difficult to achieve. What is so discouraging about the circumstances to date, however, is that the Republicans apparently have accommodated their ax-grinders with so few reservations, as the examples that Tom Moore has given illustrate so clearly.

Susan Feigenbaum: "What Role for Private Initiatives?"

As most of us would agree, the thinking behind deregulation is that the private sector can do things better—albeit still sometimes imperfectly—without government's all-too-visible hand to not-so-gently guide it. Mr. Reagan was quick to adopt this line of thought as a cornerstone of his administration; however, as Tom Moore has indicated, the present administration has been slow in eliminating regulations that were instituted previously because of interest group pressures and that serve primarily to protect industries from competition. Perhaps not surprisingly, the administration and Congress have moved with exceptional speed to kill proposed regulations and current legislation that would *reduce* some industries' insulation from market forces of competition.

I am referring primarily to regulations that monitor competitive practices and mandate industry disclosures about product quality and prices. The administration and Congress have sought to emasculate and defeat such regulatory activities targeted at the funeral and used car industries and the professions—more in response to industry pressures than to cost-benefit analyses. Recently, the FTC (Federal Trade Commission) announced that it would reassess the resources devoted to truth-in-advertisement enforcement, since "everybody can already discern when ads make patently absurd claims." Certainly the hundreds of individuals who have invested and lost large sums of money in mail-order schemes, land purchases, fast-food franchise agreements, and second trust deed markets would vehemently disagree. So would those who have suffered physical harm from tainted and improperly prepared products. Disclosure rules would facilitate information about product quality and price, thereby reducing the costs of search and potential fraud. Obviously, there is an optimal mix of industry disclosure and consumer investment in information, since industry compliance and regulatory enforcement costs can be far from negligible. However, I would argue that given industry's lower cost of access to production and price information and the high priority given by voters in recent polls to consumer protection, the optimal amount of industry mandated disclosure is not zero.

The major premise of deregulation—that the private sector can do it better—has recently been extended to apply to the government's involvement in and financing of social welfare programs, under the rubric of "private initiatives." To what degree can we realistically expect that private initiatives can be relied upon to provide Reagan's social safety net in lieu of government participation?

Clearly, there are many opportunities for elimination or redesign of regulations that have effectively impeded private initiatives. Minimum wage legislation has generated an ever-increasing need for unemployment insurance; differential Medicare reimbursement schemes for at-home versus out-of-home health care have enhanced the need for government health care expenditures; differential tax treatment for at-home versus out-of-home care of the elderly and young has led to more and more costly support systems for these dependent strata of our nation's age distribution, and it has discouraged extended family relationships. Stringent development, zoning, and occupancy laws not only reduce the incentives for private provision of low-income housing stock, but also discourage efficient utilization of the current stock by discriminating against extended and multiple family living arrangements. Eligibility rules for government support programs impose high marginal tax rates on earned incomes of the working poor and have, in the past, encouraged one-parent households. Certainly, subject to a cost-benefit evaluation, many of these regulations could be redesigned or even abolished, thereby reducing the pressures for a governmentally supported social safety net.

Furthermore, by eliminating government-subsidized prices of government goods and services and instead pricing services at cost, with desired income redistributions provided through carefully targeted voucher systems, we would expect to see a more optimal mix of public and private provision in such areas as health care and education. This mix would be further enhanced by forcing public enterprises to face the same unsubsidized input prices that their counterparts face. Currently, the use of tax-exempt borrowing instruments is one of the biggest factors accounting for cost-of-service differentials in public versus private water utilities.

What about the potential role of voluntarism and individual and corporate philanthropy in further reducing current government expenditures that have ostensibly maintained an income floor for our citizenry? In 1980, the last year we have figures for, the private philanthropic sector generated a little over $40 billion in contributions, 5 percent of that amount coming from the corporate sector. At the same time, the federal government spent over $200 billion in what were deemed "social welfare expenditures." Can the private sector be expected to undertake significantly more of the federal government's share of expenditures? My answer would be that without any further fiscal incentive than current tax deductibility, private philanthropy will continue to grow much as it has in the last decade, at slightly less than the rate of inflation. Empirical studies have indicated that private giving *would* be responsive to tax stimuli in the form of tax credits—that is, giving is price elastic. Whether this is a desirable direction in which to move, however, raises a number of complicated issues of economic efficiency and social thought. Careful study and debate are needed before major fiscal initiatives should be undertaken in this area.

I believe that the present administration can win support from lower- and middle-income voters, as well as from more liberal Democrats, for its efforts to make significant budget reductions in inefficient social welfare programs and to remove distorting user fee subsidies, *if* such modifications are accompanied by a well thought-out, comprehensive system of targeted subsidies and stimulation of the private sector. To preserve such broad-based support, however, the administration must maintain its credibility by acknowledging the limitations of private enterprise as a perfect and complete substitute for government involvement in the areas of income maintenance and regulation.

Robert Tollison: "Difficulties Facing Regulatory Reform"

In talking about the Reagan administration's approach to deregulation, we have first to remember that the independent regulatory commissions are not easy institutions to change. In fact, they were set up so they would not be easy to change. They are a hybrid kind of bureaucracy that economists have not studied in detail in trying to explain what and why they do things. They are majority-rule institutions. Decisions are often made by three-to-two votes of commissioners, who have staggered seven-year terms. Three belong to the president's party, two to the other party. The chairmen have extra power; they are the chief administrators of these bureaus. But you cannot expect the rate of change to be dramatic.

A second point concerns the Gorsuch approach to regulatory reform that Tom Moore mentioned. This involves cutting the budget and firing people, raising hell with the bureaucracy. It is quite right to focus on the output of regulatory agencies. The laws and the rules are what impose costs on the economy. But if you take the regulatory budgets, not just the independent agencies but the Agriculture, Justice, and other departmental budgets, from FY 78 to FY 81 — and that's the budget that Reagan inherited in FY 81 — those budgets increased 135 percent. They more than doubled their FY 78 level. If you look at Reagan's first two budgets, FY 82 and FY 83, those same budgets should show an aggregate increase of 3.7 percent. That is consistent with what the president has been saying. He is saying, "I haven't stopped the growth of government yet, but I have slowed it." And he has definitely slowed the growth in regulatory budgets. You need lawyers and economists to write rules, to regulate, and to have cases, and thus if you have fewer lawyers and fewer economists, you are going to have fewer rules, regulations, and cases. If you cut back the budget, you do less regulation. In fact, for a one percent increase in these budgets, you get about a two-thirds increase in the amount of regulatory activity. Therefore, you have to cut a lot to reduce regulatory activity substantially.

A third point I would make about Tom's discussion concerns Executive Order 12291. I fully agree that cost-benefit analysis is no panacea. Consider what this executive order did. It didn't just change the process. It didn't just say, "Do the cost-benefit analysis, and we will review." From a bureaucratic standpoint, it centralized the determination of costs and benefits. Under the old system, benefits were very concentrated, and costs were very diffuse. If consumers or taxpayers wanted to fight, they had to go to forums all across town. As one might predict from public choice analysis, nobody fought. Executive Order 12291 shifted the locus of these costs and benefits and tilted them in such a way that the forces of deregulation will find it more worthwhile to make themselves heard. Tom Willett has often talked about the analogy of lobbying against a single tariff, which is hardly worth anybody's time, versus lobbying against the average level of all tariffs. There is a big difference. The benefits are much higher in the second case. Executive Order 12291 may or may not work, but it is an innovation worth thinking about independently of the state of the art of cost-benefit analysis, because it essentially centralizes the benefits of seeking deregulation.

VI

Reaganomics and Income Distribution

9

MICHAEL J. BOSKIN

Distributional Effects of the Reagan Program

At the center of the Reagan administration's economic program is an attempt to limit redistribution of income to a social "safety net." The program proposes to turn us away from an evolution, partly unintentional, that was in the process of transforming our system of government fiscal devices into a general system for the redistribution of income. The administration has explicitly rejected using the tax system to tinker with the distribution of tax burdens. Instead, its policies have focused on restoring incentives in our economy to produce income and wealth and raise the *absolute level* of income on average. The administration hopes that its program will result in an environment in which economic mobility for the disadvantaged and minorities is maximized.

This effort is based on the premise that when economic growth is generally sluggish, those who have not yet made it on the economic ladder face the greatest difficulty in improving their lot. At the same time, those who cannot make it at all face a deterioration of political support for the taxes needed to finance their rescue. In short, in a stagnant economic environment, the poorest are doomed to suffer most.

In this sense, the administration's long-term strategy seems to me both sound and sensible. We do not yet have enough evidence upon which to evaluate its likely success or failure, and we are at the moment barraged with complaints from those who are forced to adjust to the likely new scenario. Yet without turning our backs on individuals and households who need to be assisted in this adjustment process, it is important that we hold to the general course. Simply put, our future standard of living depends upon restoring incentives to produce income and wealth, and this in turn depends in no small measure upon our ability to achieve a degree of control over the exploding growth of transfer payment programs that so far has eluded us.

Yet the overall Reagan program is particularly difficult to evaluate sensibly, for three reasons. First, it is just beginning. Second, it proposes a major transition to a different role for government in our society, which will inevitably have short-term painful effects. And third, we find ourselves currently evaluating long-range hopes from the bottom of a deep recession. Add to all this the fact that the program is caught up in the midst of major ideological confrontations and it becomes clear that the earliest evaluations, such as the Urban Institute's *The Reagan Experiment,*[1] can best be understood as extremely preliminary and generally short-run in focus.

Long-Run v. Short-Run Effects

Neither those who argue that virtually every item in the Reagan administration's policy disproportionately harms the disadvantaged, nor those who argue that no one will suffer in the course of this transition, are correct. One needs a modicum of historical perspective, especially to see the enormous gains made in the reduction of poverty in the United States and the enormous costs we have incurred in developing a myriad of overlapping anti-poverty programs. Misconceptions abound concerning the role of various programs in income redistribution and the alleviation of poverty or temporary hardship.

The typical analysis of the distributive effects of budget changes focuses on short-run current income. This focus inevitably ignores a host of considerations, such as the difference between permanent and transitory income; long-run versus short-run perspectives on the ultimate impact of policies; the appropriate measure of economic well-being, including a careful accounting for changing household structure and life-cycle considerations; the thorny problem of the incidence of various taxes; the equities and inequities created in comparing the net policy impacts on different groups in the population; the limitations of various government instruments in alleviating distress and/or redistributing economic well-being when private incentives to produce income and wealth may be impaired; and the problems of ethics that one encounters in even beginning to decide on an appropriate measure of economic well-being. More demagogic rhetoric than careful thought has gone into the discussion of these issues to date.

The United States has made remarkable progress in reducing poverty over the last several decades. Even the official statistics dramatically underestimate how successful, if costly, the War on Poverty has been. As late as 1962, when the official poverty index was developed, 22 percent of Americans lived in families with incomes below the poverty line. By 1980 this figure had declined to 12 percent. Thus the War on Poverty appeared half-won.

However, official poverty statistics do not include any

value whatsoever for the cash equivalent of subsidized commodities and services provided to low-income individuals. For
example, food stamps, subsidized rent, and subsidized medical care account for substantial expenditures of public funds
and a nontrivial fraction of the income of certain poor
groups, especially the elderly poor. Any reasonable attempt
to include even a conservative estimate of the cash value of
these programs suggests that the fraction of Americans living below the poverty line is actually about 5 percent.
Therefore I would characterize the general progress in
sharply curtailing the incidence of poverty in the United
States as quite successful. Despite all the problems of our income maintenance system, it is important not to forget the
single most significant thing about it: it has helped alleviate,
in an affluent if struggling economy and society, an enormous fraction of the poverty in the United States. This is one
of the greatest achievements of our society in the last several decades.

The situation is not, however, as rosy as it might seem.

The usual measure of economic well-being and income distribution is current income. The usual procedure is to array
the distribution by deciles or quartiles and analyze the share
of income accruing to individuals or households in this way.
Various statistical measures, such as Gini coefficients and
Lorenz curves, have been developed for presenting this distribution in a single figure or in graphic display.

Growth of Transfer Payments

While time-series comparisons of the distribution of income
in the United States are notoriously unreliable, it is clear
that in recent decades the poorest people have received a
substantial increase in their share of income. A large portion
comes from government transfer payment programs.

Three decades ago, transfer payments to individuals accounted for only one-seventh of the federal budget. Today,

excluding interest on the debt, transfer payments to individuals account for over half of the budget. Such payments now substantially exceed expenditures on goods and services. Figure 1 graphically displays the growth of some of these transfer payment programs and program expansions. The transfer payment programs have grown exponentially, and many of them are not very target-effective. Programs originally designed to serve the truly needy have often grown to encompass a much wider clientele and hence require much more government funding than predicted.

As table 1 suggests, the assignment of the benefits of government programs and the allocation of the burdens of taxation to different income groups suggest *at first glance* that the effect of government intervention in market outcomes on the distribution of income has been substantially to

Table 1
Net Fiscal Impact—
All Levels Of Government

Income class (in 1968 dollars)	Benefit (negative = burden) as percent of total family income[a]
$92,000	− 12%
35,500 − 92,000	− 8
22,600 − 35,500	− 9
17,500 − 22,600	− 9
12,500 − 17,500	− 7
10,400 − 12,500	− 4
7,900 − 10,400	1
5,700 − 7,900	11
4,000 − 5,700	28
4,000	96

[a]Since 1968, the huge growth of transfers would greatly increase the net benefit figures for the (inflation-adjusted) lower-income groups.

Source: R. Musgrave and P. Musgrave, *Public Finance in Theory and Practice* (New York: McGraw-Hill, 1975), based on data for 1968 and authors' preferred assumptions.

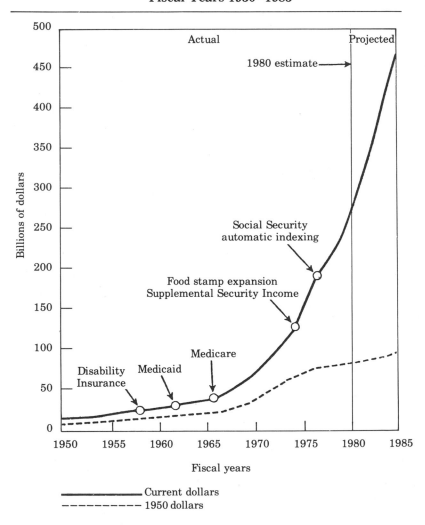

Figure 1
Outlays for Benefit Payments for Individuals,
Fiscal Years 1950–1985

redistribute income toward the lower tail of the income distribution from the upper tail.

It is important to realize that the government began its efforts to eradicate poverty and reduce the harm of temporary economic disruptions such as unemployment or ill health at a time of very rapid general economic growth. In the quarter century following World War II, real per capita GNP in the United States increased at 2.4 percent per year, as opposed to the long-term historical growth rate of slightly under 2 percent. At such growth rates, real incomes approximately doubled between generations: each generation was approximately twice as wealthy over its lifetime as the generation that preceded it. This made it quite easy to share generously with the less fortunate in society.

Unfortunately, the general economy has been rocked by a series of problems in recent years. In the last decade the overwhelming bulk of working, taxpaying American families have seen virtually no gain in their standard of living. Real GNP per capita growth has been cut by more than a half since the original Arab oil embargo of 1973. Worse yet, most of this growth in real GNP can be accounted for by the enormous expansion of the labor force in this period: the post–World War II baby boom generation came of working age, and many more married women became employed. Real income per worker per hour in this period did not grow at all; in fact, average real spendable earnings have fallen since 1967. The last several recessions, the huge transfer of income to OPEC, and the distressing long-term productivity slowdown have all greatly changed the environment for support of income maintenance program extensions—let alone general income redistribution. It is not surprising that increased demands for more target-effective and cost-conscious entitlement programs have emerged. Indeed, it is now widely recognized that in the 1970s the poor gained in real income relative to the general population. For example, real Social Security benefits increased by 28 percent between 1969 and 1979, whereas average after-tax real wages fell.

In order to finance the growth of these transfer payment programs, average and marginal tax rates increased substantially. The insidious interaction of inflation and our unindexed tax system left us by the end of the 1970s with the greatest proportion of Americans in history subject to high effective marginal tax rates on incremental earnings or investment income. It is the marginal, or incremental, tax rate that most influences work effort, saving and investment, and risk taking.

How Much Redistribution?

A variety of important issues emerge concerning attempts to redistribute income and/or provide income security for those unable to provide for themselves. It is generally recognized that in a market-oriented society earnings will primarily reflect productivity. Since in the United States the overwhelming bulk of income accrues as earnings and fringe benefits (over 75 percent in recent years), as opposed to the returns to investment income, most inequality of wealth is due to the unequal distribution of earnings.

Even in a world where everyone started out with the same earnings potential, a variety of factors would certainly lead to inequality in earnings outcomes. In an uncertain world, various factors affect the demand for different skills in the labor force. Also, the distribution of ill health or other temporary impairments is certainly very uneven. Perhaps most important, parental and educational influences vary substantially.

It is also clear that individuals differ considerably in their potential earnings capacity in ways that are not wholly related to differences in educational achievement or early childhood parental input. In a primitive society, relying heavily on hunting ability for provision of food, those who are fleet of foot, strong, and with good eyesight undoubtedly flourish relative to those who have none of these attributes.

In our society, however difficult it is to measure, other attributes that are highly correlated with earnings ability—intelligence, savvy, or whatever—are differentially distributed. There is also the factor of luck.

In recent years a number of attempts have been made to place these kinds of issues in a more formal context. Sometimes going under the heading of "optimal taxation," these analyses attempt to integrate into a careful analysis of the optimal tax/transfer system various features of the distribution of abilities, the degree of ethical concern for unequal outcomes, and government's ability to redistribute income in a relatively decentralized society in which individuals are free to choose the amount of work effort they supply to the market, their human investment, their saving, investment, and risk taking, etc. These analyses reveal a variety of important conclusions. Except under very extreme concern for relative as opposed to absolute income levels,[2] even the most egalitarian of social ethics—the belief that society ought to maximize the well-being of the worst off (sometimes called the Rawlsian or "maxi-min" criterion)—does not lead to substantial income redistribution when the economic distortions lead to severe efficiency losses; moreover, the need for prohibitive tax rates can lead to reduced tax revenues available for the redistribution.

Further, it is important to note that government "failure" often occurs in the attempt to redistribute income or economic well-being. First, there arises the usual problem of deadweight loss or inefficiency of the tax system in resource allocation, e.g., between consumption and saving or work and leisure. Also, there can be considerable mistargeting of the funds raised to redistribute income. In addition, programs can require substantial administrative costs. Each of these problems can make the per-dollar equivalent received by a low-income individual much more costly than a dollar at the margin in large redistribution programs.

It is also worth noting the potential impact of the recent

trend toward providing in-kind commodities rather than
cash. This may be motivated by a desire of the population to
take care of individuals' basic needs.[3] Direct provision of
education, health, food, etc., may generate substantially
more public support than providing income in general for the
poor. However, direct-provision programs may, via the in-
genuity of the recipients, end up merely redistributing income in roughly cash equivalent form. This occurs when programs have a marginal copayment, or a cap or ceiling. For
example, paying a certain amount per dollar of food stamps
effectively rations their use only when the total amount of
food purchases would have been less than the available
amount of food stamps. When it is greater, the food stamps
no longer operate at the margin, and their cash equivalent
value is similar in its potential impacts on economic behavior
to a general cash grant for the relevant amount.

Thus, incentives are important not only in their potential
impact on those financing redistributive or income security
programs, but also in their impact on the behavior of those
receiving the benefits.

Finally, we come to the critically important and hugely
controversial general question of what role the government
should take in redistributing wealth. To what extent is it
legitimate for government to attempt a *general* redistribution of income or economic well-being? Should the government's role instead be limited to (at most) alleviating poverty
and mitigating the harm of temporary economic distress? It
is certainly the case that there is a good deal of public concern with disproportionate accumulations of income and
wealth. However, it is my opinion that in a society with an
average income level as high as ours, the primary goal of
government policy ought to be—and the overwhelming bulk
of citizens may be expected to support—substantial relief for
those at the lower end of the income distribution. This moral
mandate simply does not extend to attempts to redistribute
minor amounts of the tax burden from the fifth to the fourth

decile of the income distribution. It is my opinion that there is substantial public support for anti-poverty programs and cost-effective social insurance, but not for a general redistributive pattern of taxation and benefit payments.

The Life-Cycle View

A substantial amount of research now indicates that many economic decisions, including a variety of those relating to consumption, saving, human investment, etc., are at least partially determined by *long-term* considerations of expected returns, costs, and risks. This life-cycle profile indicates increasing earnings, albeit at a decreasing rate, until late in working life, and then a substantial reduction in earnings as individuals reach age 60 and beyond. The permanent income or life-cycle view has a variety of important implications for discussing issues of income distribution.

First, it is important to note that data for any individual year will contain some individuals or households who have temporarily high or low income relative to their long-run average. Also, failing to disaggregate to narrow age cohorts confuses the picture. It is only natural that there should be concentration of earnings, or income, by age, since more experienced workers are generally more productive and hence better paid. Thus, whatever degree of inequality is measured in the distribution of individual year data on income probably overstates substantially the degree of inequality relative to some longer-term average.

Second, taking the somewhat long-term perspective also raises the question of mobility for individuals or households within the earnings or income distribution over some span of time, perhaps even as long as their lifetime. Recent analyses of longitudinal data suggest that there is a good deal of such mobility.

Third, the life-cycle or permanent income theory suggests that consumption may be a better measure of long-run economic well-being than is current income. This is true for a number of reasons. Most important, the fact that people's consumption patterns reflect their expected future income fluctuations suggests that consumption may be a better measure of *permanent* income than is current income.

Fourth, it is important to account for the fact that consumption, and also a certain amount of production of economic activity, occurs in households. Given the major changes in the composition of the U.S. population in terms of age, marriage, divorce, average family size, etc., it is important for measurements of economic well-being to be standardized for family size, without losing sight of the fact that family size is subject to the choice of individuals and can vary over the course of an individual's lifetime.

Fifth, there have in fact been econometric studies of the determinants of earnings adjusted for some of the above life-cycle effects. It turns out that education, experience, hours of work, and a variety of other factors explain a substantial amount—perhaps 40 percent—of the variation in observed earnings. Much of the effect of education works through occupation and industry. Therefore, it is likely that policies that affect the distribution of educational attainment, properly measured, will affect the ultimate distribution of earnings outcomes. This has become an important issue in a variety of discussions concerning school expenditures and financing. While much debate remains concerning whether or how educational outcomes can be affected by altering educational input, a real effort has been made to equalize expenditures on public education. Of course, there have been well-known attempts at private offsets to this. While the end results of different educational expenditure policies are not yet determined, it is clear that the government's ability to affect educational outcomes (and hence the distribution of wealth) is likely to be rather severely circumscribed. A critical limiting factor may well be the "cycle of poverty."

Simply put, for a given level of income guarantee, or level

of generosity for those at the very bottom, either we have a very large fraction of the population receiving some income transfers, or we have high marginal tax rates that reduce the incentive of those receiving the transfer payments at the bottom of the income scale to go out and find market work. This fundamental dilemma has led to the categorization of individuals, rather than to a broad definition of eligibility based exclusively on income, in order to target help (the disabled, mothers with dependent children, etc.).

The broader issue that is raised by these questions concerns the trade-offs of reliance on the market versus faith in government programs. This moves beyond the scope of the present analysis. Taking the narrow economic income or consumption measure of well-being may ignore important psychological, sociological, and political interactions of government transfer recipients—as well as those paying taxes to finance them—with the economic system. Such issues as the "stigma" of welfare, the "distrust or disgust" with government, etc., are undoubtedly important in evaluating primarily market-based outcomes and/or particular government programs and their alternatives.

The Reagan Program: Some Preliminary Analysis

With the exception of its short-term macroeconomic consequences, no aspect of the Reagan administration's program has received more attention than its likely effect on income distribution. It has been repeatedly attacked for its perceived inequity and unfairness. This has been the case in debate over each and every item of the program, as well as in evaluating the program as a whole. Before we address these issues directly, it is important to note that the program is not yet fully in place: there is substantial doubt concerning the extent of future benefit growth reductions and revisions in the original tax program, etc. It is also important to point out that as passed by Congress and signed into law, the original budget and tax programs—which have received the most attention—did not coincide precisely with the administration's program. I do not propose here to delve into such distinctions, but merely to highlight some general perspectives on economic effects. The fact that there was pressure from the House of Representatives that led to the immediate reduction of the top tax rates on investment income from 70 percent to 50 percent, or that a variety of the spending reductions originally requested were not passed, or that the Social Security proposals were rebuffed virtually instantaneously, and so forth, will not occupy us here in attempting to assign credit or blame.

Most of the attacks have been simply misdirected. This is because virtually all analyses have focused almost exclusively on the distribution of *short-run disposable income*, and related activity. No clear benchmark has been delineated in evaluating the programs' potential equity effects. For example, any specific reduction in spending growth has been evaluated relative to how that spending growth would have continued under the Carter administration's proposals. Usually ignored is how we were going to finance that additional growth and the economic effects of failing to do so. It is true that any substantial change in fiscal policy '(or monetary or regulatory policy as well) will lead to a substantial short-term disruption in many households. That much is clear. The overall administration program, however, attempts to change the role of government in our economy. The goal is to achieve a smaller relative size of the federal government, shifting some responsibilities to the state and local levels while relying on the private sector for other activity and simply eliminating certain programs for those other than the truly needy. In addition, major tax reductions, heavily focused on marginal tax rates, are designed to restore incentives to produce income and wealth and help restore our long-term productivity growth with the hope of raising incomes in general.

The times of the most rapid gains in the relative incomes of the poor and the minorities in the United States have been those of rapid general economic growth. Thus a painful dilemma arises as we are forced to choose between substantially increasing the level of well-being of future minority and low-income households versus the short-run harm of disrupting households that have become relatively dependent on transfer payment income.

The archetypical analysis of the distributional impacts of the program cross-classifies households by current income categories and estimates the change in their tax payments, or benefits received under a particular set of programs, relative to what they would have been had a different scenario been followed. However, the implications of that other scenario for our long-term growth, inflation, etc., are usually not spelled out. In such analyses it is clear that a nontrivial number of households would be subject to short-term income cuts. This does not itself constitute an indictment. Instead, it merely reflects the administration's attempts to make a variety of programs more target-effective. For example, many in-kind transfer payment programs have had their eligibility standards tightened from almost twice to only one and one-third times the poverty line.

The major "casualties" will be those who will have to move to greater dependence on earnings-related income in order to maintain their current level of consumption, although certainly some will reduce work in order to retain eligibility. This involves real hardship. However, it is also important to point out that these individuals and households in general benefited substantially as these programs grew to serve a much wider clientele than originally intended. Nobody likes to see his economic situation worsen, even temporarily, but the growth of the federal budget on such transfer payment programs was so rapid that its financing threatened to erode private incentives and eventually to crowd out virtually all other government purchases of goods and services.

The administration aptly sums up its approach to altering redistributive spending programs with the notion of a social "safety net." It has focused heavily on preserving programs for the "truly needy" and has explicitly rejected general redistribution to the nonpoor. Many of the nonpoor currently receiving benefits will certainly suffer in the interim. Also, there may be an incentive for some of those slightly above the new eligibility criteria to reduce their earnings or alter their activities in other ways to become eligible. But certainly the intent of the proposals is to reduce the fraction of Americans receiving transfer payment income in the United States. The hope is that, combined with a variety of other actions, this will lead to an eventually higher level of income, whether or not it improves the distribution of this potentially higher income.

Effects of Tax Cuts

On the tax side, much attention has focused on the fact that higher-income people would receive more in reduced taxes via the administration's program than would lower-income individuals. As pointed out by myself and others, this results primarily from the fact that higher-income people already pay higher taxes. The personal income tax cut is approximately an equal percent reduction in tax payments—so the distribution of wealth would not be much altered.

The most important question about the tax cuts concerns their potential effects on various other aspects of economic activity, *contingent on a given spending and monetary policy.* It is possible that the overall fiscal policy might lead to a different short- or long-term level of economic activity than would have occurred otherwise, but this again is problematical to forecast. The single most redistributive aspect of the personal tax cut was the reduction of the maximum tax on investment income from 70 percent to 50 percent. Yet this is probably the structural feature of the tax code that is likely to yield the least revenue loss per dollar of potential investment and saving stimulus. Not very much tax revenue was collected at these rates, as a percentage of the total, and an enormous distortion of economic activity into tax shelters and perhaps under-reporting also occurred. It is important to realize that the individuals involved were paying "implicit" taxes via reduced returns in other activities in order to achieve this tax sheltering. Hence, their effective total burden—tax plus reduced return—was substantially larger than the tax revenue collected. This part of the tax change is highly worthwhile because it has reduced distortion of investment with only a modest reduction, if any, in tax revenues. Also, the effect of a tighter monetary policy on asset values, especially housing, has been to create large capital losses for owners of these assets, who are disproportionately wealthy.

The business side of the tax cut has received much attention, but once again we must repeat what I and others have said so many times before, that businesses are merely complex conduits for economic activity and that all taxes are ultimately paid by individuals and households. Whether corporate taxes are paid for by corporate shareholders, by capital owners in general, or partly by consumers is a thorny problem in tax incidence. Suffice it to say that the substantial reductions in corporate income taxes—embodied in the accelerated cost recovery system and other features of the Economic Recovery Tax Act of 1981—are in part merely an adjustment for the failure to index for inflation and for a substantial reduction in real net rates of return on investment income in the 1970s. Also, while not entirely eliminating the inflation distortion from income tax, or moving us to neutrality in the investment/consumption choice (as would a properly implemented expenditure tax), the reductions probably do move us in the right direction in this regard. Since income from capital, which bears much of the burden of the corporate tax, is disproportionately received by those in up-

per income brackets (although not as disproportionately as
would be revealed by looking at data for an individual year or
short period), these reductions should reduce tax burdens on
the wealthy more than on low-income individuals. However,
in our complicated political economy the likely effects of
these tax reductions are to leave greater income in the hands
of the private sector, hopefully stimulating capital formation
and the level of future income in general.

The taxing and spending changes made by the administration will move us toward a society with a smaller fraction of
its population dependent on transfer payment programs.
They will encourage increased productivity for workers of
the future and hence stimulate earnings growth. It is
generally believed, although very poorly documented, that
low-income individuals are hurt disproportionately by inflation. It is certainly true that high inflation interacts with our
tax system and our investment decisions to become an ob-
stacle to long-term growth, and it is quite likely, in the long
run, that no group in society has a greater stake than
workers in reducing the rate of inflation. In any case, the indexing and a variety of other features of transfer payments
suggest that in the course of high and fluctuating inflation in
the 1970s, individuals in the lowest part of the income distribution received increases in their real income from
transfer payments that went well beyond the general income
growth in society. Further, since average real spendable
earnings declined in this decade, the distribution of post-
tax and post-transfer real spendable earnings was made
more equal.

The single most important redistributive device is the
Social Security system. Social Security benefits are projected
to exceed $170 billion next year, and taxes to finance them
grow apace. The program has a long-term unfunded net
liability larger than the privately held national debt. The
system not only transfers income from the current generation of workers to the current generation of retirees, but also

attempts substantial redistribution within the specific age cohorts. This occurs because of the progressive nature of the benefit formula, the payment of spouses', widows', and various other dependents' benefits, etc. The Social Security system provides the most flagrant willy-nilly redistributions of income from those of modest means to those who are well-off. Since we generally define eligibility for Social Security very broadly, and blanket in virtually everybody for the auxiliary benefits *regardless of need,* many of the benefits originally intended to serve a particularly distressing need have grown to encompass millions of individuals who are by no means needy. The funeral benefit is particularly apropos: originally designed to prevent the indecency of a widow's not being able to bury her deceased spouse, the program now applies to all individuals eligible for Social Security. Thus even a millionaire's widow is eligible for funeral benefits.

Unfortunately, Social Security is so difficult to explain, and so politically charged, that this administration, as most others, has found it difficult to achieve any cost savings in a target-effective manner. While the original proposals had many worthwhile ideas, the one feature of substantially reducing the benefits for those who retire prior to age 65 received such adverse attention that the similarity of the administration's well thought-out program proposals with those of the House Ways and Means Social Security Sub-Committee's own reform package received little attention. So large are the sums involved in Social Security, and so potentially vast are its interactions with a variety of other aspects of our economy, that the failure to reform it has been the single most important disappointment in the current economic program.

Unfortunately, time is running out for sensible long-term reform in Social Security. Shortly after the baby boom generation retires early in the next century, the ratio of retirees to workers will increase by about 75 percent. This not only will place enormous financial pressure on the pay-as-you-go financed Social Security system, but probably will make it politically impossible to implement any sensible reform procedures. Since it is generally agreed that structural reform in Social Security must be implemented gradually and after a grace period, so as not to deprive current beneficiaries, the reform process must begin soon.

Absolute v. Relative Gains

Unquestionably, the Reagan economic program will lead to a more unequal distribution of income than would have resulted from a continuation of previous programs. But to criticize it on this basis would be an error. We had made such substantial, if incomplete, progress in eliminating poverty and providing social insurance against various income losses that the returns from such distribution were diminishing rapidly while the costs were disproportionately accelerating. The move for further substantial redistribution via the tax system, along with major growth in transfer programs, is in my opinion no longer politically or economically sustainable. The move to restructure our policies in an attempt to achieve greater productivity growth and less dependence on government assistance augurs well not only for the long-run health of the general economy, but also for the opportunities available to the least well-off in our society for increasing their real income. Only those firmly committed to an exclusive focus on the relative income of low-income individuals, as opposed to their absolute living standard, would ignore these long-term benefits in evaluating "Reaganomics."

RESPONSE

Henry J. Aaron: "Raising Some Doubts"

To assess the distributional effects of the Reagan economic program, it is important to begin by making clear what one means by the Reagan economic program. I define it as a combination of greatly reduced nondefense spending, greatly increased defense spending, greatly reduced business taxes, somewhat reduced personal taxes, and tight money. In combination, these policies have a variety of effects—on aggregate demand, on aggregate supply, on the composition of demand, on factor shares, on disposable personal incomes, and on the flow of public services. Each of these effects has distributional consequences. Michael Boskin's paper stresses, correctly, that sorting out all of the distributional effects of each of the elements of the economic program via each of these channels is a very complex problem and that few have illuminated it.

To do so it would be necessary either to trace the consequences of the several elements of the economic program on distribution or to analyze in some detail the distributional consequences of one or a few elements, taking all others for granted. In passing, I would question whether, having considered Boskin's paper, many of you have a clear idea of how he thinks Reagan's program will affect the economic prospects of, say, the poor or blacks, or whether the aged will gain or lose. I am sure that I do not. The reason, quite simply, is that he never tells us with what the Reagan program is being compared. It is not enough to wave one's hands and assert that the alternative was "more of the same." Almost everyone agreed last year that the growth of public spending needed to be cut and that business taxation needed to be reformed. The critical questions that were and are before

Congress, the president, the Federal Reserve, and the American people concern how far to push various policies and in what combination. At the same time, it is not legitimate to say that we do not know what the Reagan program is. The president's program may not become the nation's if Congress modifies or rejects the administration's proposals. But the president has made us all understand what he wants.

If we were to pursue a macroeconomic approach to analyzing the effects of the Reagan program on distribution, we should conclude that in the *short run* the program unambiguously helps recipients of capital income at the expense of recipients of labor income, and the wealthy at the expense of the poor. The outcome of the heavy reliance on tight money, combined with much-enlarged deficits, both now and for the foreseeable future, and with tax cuts that taken alone tend to increase the demand for capital, has been increased real interest rates and reduced demand for labor. As always, increased unemployment falls with particular severity on low-income and minority workers. In the *long run,* these effects may be reversed, *if* other public policies do not offset these results.

But the long run can be very long. Neither the administration nor Mike Boskin has presented evidence establishing that such equalizing results will actually occur or how long will pass before they become apparent. They assert these results as matters of faith. Thus, as far as the flow of factor incomes is concerned, the short- and intermediate-term effects of the budget are regressive; the long-run effects depend on so many factors that one can get almost any prediction depending on the model one chooses and the parameters one selects for it.

Turning to the effect of the Reagan tax and spending changes on real disposable income reinforces these findings. The best that can be said for the personal income tax cuts — and the administration has said it often—is that they were roughly proportional with respect to tax liability; but they were clearly regressive with respect to disposable personal income. Furthermore, this comparison leaves entirely out of account the business tax cuts that accrue almost exclusively to upper-bracket individuals under any extant short-run incidence theory. In this connection, Boskin's statement that the business tax cuts offset the unjustified increase in business taxes attributable to inflation is true only for inflation rates of roughly 10 to 12 percent. If inflation falls to 6 percent or less, the combination of the investment tax credit and the modified 10-5-3 plan passed by Congress converts the corporation tax into an investment subsidy for new depreciable investments. Moreover, as the Council of Economic Advisers so deftly showed in its report this year, the tax bill produces effective tax rates that vary capriciously and without rationale across industries. Business taxation badly needed reform, but in 1981 the administration proposed a poor reform and Congress, with bipartisan ineptitude, made it worse.

On the expenditure side of the budget, the direct impact of President Reagan's requests, enacted in part last year and extended in the 1983 budget, is clear and simple. Defense outlays and interest payments increase. Social Security is reduced, but only a little. The bulk of the reductions occur in nondefense outlays, in programs that disproportionately serve various target populations: the aged, disabled, and survivors; blacks and other minorities; the handicapped; the poor; students in school districts with many poor kids; the unemployed; and other groups.

These programs have grown in the last two decades, although not nearly so rapidly as the entitlements; but budget cuts fall most heavily on them. Many of the programs needed badly to be reformed. But we should be clear who loses when they are cut. This list makes clear that the references to the poor or truly needy divert attention from the original purpose of these programs. They were not intended to help the poor, per se; they were intended to equalize educational opportunity, to offer social services to target groups, to provide legal representation for those who lacked it, and so on.

We should also be clear that these cuts are not the regrettable but necessary sacrifices to reduce inflation or increase productivity. No evidence has been presented that progress in cutting inflation or boosting productivity will be slowed if defense spending is a bit lower or taxes a bit higher than Mr. Reagan has requested and the available funds are used to offer legal services for the poor, enriched primary education for poor kids (which evaluations now show to increase educational performance), or grants for low-income college students. As Boskin points out, it is at this level, rather than at the global level of the general income distribution, that political interest in the United States has focused; and it is at this level that we should appraise the distributional effects of the Reagan economic program.

We can have a smaller government, if that is what we want, but we do not have to get it with a combination of tax cuts and expenditure cuts chosen as if to maximize the pain for those groups that suffer most from the slack economy we now find necessary to fight inflation.

In closing, let me correct one technical error in Boskin's paper. Although early articles on optimal taxation did suggest that maximization of social welfare and significant redistribution were inconsistent, this conclusion has collapsed as empirically supported estimates of labor supply have been introduced. More important, it is just plain irresponsible to make statements about practical issues from a framework so rarified and abstract and that fails so completely to represent major reasons for redistribution as does the optimal tax model.

VII

Conclusion

10

Wm. CRAIG STUBBLEBINE
THOMAS D. WILLETT

Future Directions

As should be evident from the views expressed in this volume, Reaganomics is complex and many-faceted—which in itself explains much difference of opinion concerning the administration's program. The political debate has not always reflected this complexity, and there has been a strong and understandable tendency to judge the program's performance simply in light of the administration's own early promises. By this narrow criterion, the verdict is clear: the economic miracle promised by the radical supply-siders has not come to pass.

But judged against the standards of traditional economic analysis, the outcome looks more complicated, and generally more positive. The fight against inflation is being won—in fact, more rapidly than most forecasters expected, albeit with the associated costs of a severe recession. If by exhorting us to "stay the course," the administration is warning against premature reinflation of the economy, then many economic analysts would probably join the chorus. Indeed, one of the more significant political developments in recent times has been the growing recognition, among economists and world leaders alike, that reestablishment of essential price stability is a necessary condition for regaining sustained full employment and a satisfactory rate of economic growth.

And, in fact, there continues to be broad public support for cutting the growth rates of both taxes and government spending while at the same time strengthening our national defense. But there is considerable disagreement over specifics. In the absence of a supply-side miracle, the vexing question of priorities has come to the fore. By supporting the 1982 tax increase legislation, President Reagan has made clear that the administration recognizes these difficulties and is not still wedded to the hope that supply-side wonderwork might make hard choices unnecessary. This clear signal has had the salutary effect, in many quarters, of bolstering confidence in the administration's overall program.

It is only a first step, however. A major effort will still be required to reduce further the huge long-run deficits built into the current budgets—without at the same time fundamentally sacrificing our defense buildup or reducing intolerably the levels of public services or support for the needy. The looming crisis in Social Security further complicates this problem and must be a major focus of policymakers' attention.

Contributors to this report on Reaganomics have no magic solutions to offer, but there are several points that should be kept in mind.

With regard to weighing the effectiveness of particular programs against their costs, it is important that no major area of government be exempt or appear to be exempt from close scrutiny. This is particularly important in the case of trade and regulatory policy. The administration's record on trade and regulatory liberalization has been quite mixed, and it is essential that more balanced assessments of costs and benefits be applied. In the area of defense spending, there is concern whether the defense budget has been subjected to sufficiently stringent evaluation. If the consensus for defense spending is to survive, this concern must be addressed, which means that defense expenditures must be subjected—and appear to the public to be subjected—to high standards of management review.

A second point is that disillusionment with radical supply-side economics should not deflect attention from the critical effects that government policies have on economic incentives. There are still substantial distortions and disincentive effects built into the tax code. For reasons both of equity and efficiency, tax reform needs to be given more attention. We still need a more effective structure of fiscal incentives to stimulate investment. While recent tax measures have reduced the net amount of double taxation of investment, our current tax codes still do not adequately neutralize the tax effects of varying rates of inflation, and they have created tremendous differences in the incentives to invest across different industries. Likewise, a good "flat-rate" tax system would go a long way toward reducing the perverse effects of high marginal income tax rates.

There is also a need for structural reform of the budgetary process. The current process appears to be biased toward overspending. Viewed from the perspective of public choice analysis, individual members of Congress typically appear to have stronger incentives to support than to oppose spending increases. The same structural tendencies that led to rapid increases in government spending now frustrate attempts to bring spending under better control. The proposed balanced budget amendment is designed to help solve this problem by restructuring voting procedures in a way that brings out more clearly the costs of particular programs. Whatever the ultimate fate of that particular proposal, congressional voting incentives need to be somehow reshaped.

Finally, citizens generally need to be more aware of the long-term consequences of economic policy. In the past, the attention of voters tended to focus heavily on short-run economic performance and on immediate problems such as unemployment. There are signs now that this focus is altering. This is a very healthy development. For without a high level of public awareness of the long-term challenges facing us, the prospects either for controlling federal budget growth or for restoring a stable economy will be slim indeed.

Notes

Contributors

Index

NOTES

2. Thomas D. Willett: "Fighting Stagflation: Macroeconomics under Reagan"

1. Without necessarily implying their agreement with all portions of this paper, the author would like to thank King Banaian, David Berson, James Lehman, Tom Mayer, Harold McClure, and Richard Sweeney for helpful comments on earlier versions.

2. For recent discussion of the costs of high and volatile inflation rates, see Gardner Ackley, "The Costs of Inflation," *American Economic Review,* May 1978; and Deborah Frohman, Leroy O. Laney, and Thomas D. Willett, "Uncertainty Costs of High Inflation," *Voice,* Federal Reserve Bank of Dallas, July 1981, pp. 1–9.

3. A number of prominent economists who are not supply-siders have argued against increasing taxes now. For a representative range of reactions on this issue, see Michael Evans, Martin Feldstein, Arthur Laffer, Robert Lekachman, and George Perry, "Three Cheers, Bronx Cheers for the Reagan Stance," *Los Angeles Times,* 31 January 1982; Martin Feldstein, "The Job of Reducing the Federal Deficit," *The Wall Street Journal,* 19 January 1982; Walter Heller, "Way Out of the Nation's Economic Trap," *The Wall Street Journal,* 25 February 1982; and Arthur B. Laffer, "Debunking Balanced-Budget Myths," *Los Angeles Times,* 29 December 1981.

4. Leroy Laney and Thomas D. Willett, "Presidential Politics, Budget Deficits, and Monetary Policy in the United States: 1960–1976," Claremont working paper, 1981; forthcoming in *Public Choice.*

5. Herbert Stein, "The Economy: Why I Am For Tax Increase," *The Wall Street Journal,* 5 January 1982. See also Herbert Stein, "Why Deficits Matter," *AEI Economist,* January 1982.

6. A useful recent discussion of ways to achieve greater credibility is given in Herbert Stein, "Achieving Credibility," in *Contemporary Economic Problems,* ed. William Feller (Washington, D.C.: American Enterprise Institute, 1981), pp. 39–76. One type of approach that should be studied carefully is a Constitutional amendment instituting spending limits on a balanced budget, proposals for which are currently before Congress.

7. See, for example, Robert Gordon, "What Can Stabilization Policy Achieve?" *American Economic Review,* May 1978; and idem, "Inflation, Flexible Exchange Rates, and the National Rate of Unemployment," working paper, Northwestern University and National Bureau of Economic Research, 29 May 1981.

8. For recent discussions of the cases for shock treatments versus gradualism, see William Fellner, "Introductory Remarks on Demand Disinflation: What If Gradualism Should Fail Despite Its Merits," in *Contemporary Economic Problems,* ed. William Fellner (Washington, D.C.: American Enterprise Institute, 1980); and William Fellner, Stanley Fischer, Armin Gutowski, and Rudolph Penner, *Shock Theory or Gradualism?* Group of Thirty, Occasional Paper no. 8 (New York, 1981).

9. While many economists such as Walter Heller ("Way Out of the Nation's Economic Trap," *The Wall Street Journal,* 25 February 1982) continue to believe that such a policy is feasible, the recent CEA report is quite skeptical.

10. See, for example, Thomas D. Willett and John E. Mullen, "The Effects of Alternative International Monetary Systems on Macroeconomic Discipline and the Political Business Cycle," in *The Political Economy of National and International Monetary Policy,* ed. R. Lombra and W. Witte (Ames, Iowa: Iowa State University Press, 1982), and references cited therein.

11. See C. Fred Bergsten, "The Costs of Reaganomics," *Foreign Policy* (Fall 1981): 24–36.

12. For surveys of the published literature and new results, see Jacob Dreyer, Gottfried Haberler, and Thomas D. Willett, eds., *The International Monetary System* (Washington, D.C.: American Enterprise Institute, 1982).

13. I have recently evaluated in some detail the arguments that inflationary biases exist and the major proposals for dealing with them in Thomas D. Willett, "A New Monetary Constitution? An Evaluation of the Need and the Major Alternatives," Claremont working paper, 1981; forthcoming in Alvin Rabushka and Wm. Craig Stubblebine, eds., *Constraining Federal Taxing and Spending* (Palo Alto, Calif.: Hoover Institution Press).

14. Lester Thurow has recently argued in support of this view in "Give Reagan the Fed," *Newsweek,* 1 March 1982, p. 29.

15. This is in fact one of the major majority recommendations of the recent report of the Gold Commission to Congress.

3. Richard W. Rahn: "Supply-Side Economics: The U.S. Experience"

1. Norman B. Ture, "'Supply-Side' Economics and Public Policy," testimony presented to the Joint Economic Committee, Congress of the United States, 21 May 1980, p. 1.

2. Adam Smith, *An Inquiry into the Nature and Causes of the Wealth of Nations,* ed. Edwin Cannan (Chicago: University of Chicago Press, 1976), pp. 351–52.

3. Paul Craig Roberts, "Dawdling with Incentives," *Wall Street Journal,* 7 August 1980.

4. Bruce Bartlett, *Reaganomics: Supply-Side Economics in Action* (Westport, Conn.: Arlington House, 1981), p. 116.

5. Statement before the Joint Economic Committee, Congress of the United States, 7 February 1977.

6. Richard W. Rahn and Mari Lee Dunn, "An Analysis of Tax Revenue Impacts Resulting from Changes in Capital Gains Tax Rates," *Atlantic Economic Journal* 7 (December 1979): 65.

7. *The Capital Gains Tax Cut Did Work* (Washington, D.C.: American Council for Capital Formation, 1 April 1981).

8. Arnold C. Harberger demonstrated this point in his seminal paper, "The Incidence of the Corporation Income Tax," *Journal of Political Economy,* June 1962, pp. 215–40. Harberger calculated that corporate income imposed a substantial welfare loss on the economy.

Using somewhat different approaches, Arnold Harberger and John B. Shoven, "The Incidence and Efficiency Effects of Taxes on Income from Capital," pt. 2, *Journal of Political Economy,* April 1978, pp. S29–S52, have each estimated the welfare cost from misallocation of resources caused by the corporate income tax at roughly 0.5 percent of national income.

J. Gregory Ballentine and Charles E. McClure, Jr., extended Harberger's methodology in "Taxation and Corporate Financial Policy," *Quarterly Journal of Economics,* March 1980, pp. 351–72. They conclude that "full integration, dividend-only integration, and abolition of the corporation income tax all lower the cost of equity capital for corporations. This tends to raise the rate of return to capital in the economy" (p. 370). See also references cited there.

9. Charles Becker and Don Fullerton, "Income Tax Incentives to Promote Saving," *Working Paper Series,* Working Paper No. 487 (Cambridge, Mass.: National Bureau of Economic Research, June 1980), p. 27.

10. Otto Eckstein, "A Time for Supply-Side Economics," testimony before the Joint Economic Committee, Congress of the United States, 21 May 1980.

11. New York Stock Exchange, Office of Economic Research, "Building a Better Future: Economic Choices for the 1980s," December 1979.

12. Norman B. Ture, "Capital Formation and Productivity," n.p., 1973, p. 27.

13. Douglas H. Joines, "The Kennedy Tax Cuts: An Application of the Ellipse" (Los Angeles: Arthur B. Laffer Associates, 25 September 1980), p. 6, citing Don Fullerton's "On the Possibility of an Inverse Relationship between Tax Rates and Government Revenues," *Working Paper Series,* Working Paper No. 467 (Cambridge, Mass.: National Bureau of Economic Research, April 1980); Terrence J. Wales, "Estimation of a Labor Supply Curve for Self-Employed Business Proprietors," *International Economic Review* 14 (February 1973): 69–80; and A. B. Laffer, "Prohibitive Tax Rates and the Inner-City: A Rational Explanation of the Poverty Trap," H. C. Wainwright & Co., 27 June 1978.

4.   J. Harold McClure and Thomas D. Willett: "Understanding the Supply-Siders"

1. At a recent Western Economic Association meeting on Reaganomics, Larry Kimball suggested the label "media supply-siders" for this school, as opposed to "academic supply-siders" such as Boskin, Feldstein, and Dale Jorgenson.

2. For example, both Paul Craig Roberts and Norman Ture, Reagan's former assistant and under secretary of the Treasury, argue that the proposition that tax cuts will pay for themselves is not an essential part of their version of supply-side economics. They do argue that tax cuts will be anti-inflationary, in contrast to the traditional Keynesian view that they have little effect on inflation. See, for example, the discussions in Bruce R. Bartlett, *Reaganomics* (New York: Quill, 1982), especially chapters

1–4, 10–11, and 18; Norman Ture, "Supply-Side Analysis and Public Policy," in David G. Raboy, ed., *Essays in Supply Side Economics* (Washington, D.C.: Institute for Research on the Economics of Taxation, 1982); and George Gilder, *Wealth and Poverty* (New York: Bantam, 1981).

3. The proposition that Reaganomics depends upon mainstream supply-side economics does not imply that all mainstream supply-siders will support the Reagan economic policies.

4. For discussion and references, see Bartlett, op. cit.; Michael Boskin, "Some Issues in Supply-Side Economics," in Karl Brunner and Allan H. Metzler, eds., *Supply Shock Incentives and National Wealth*, vol. 14 (Amsterdam: North-Holland Press, 1981); Henry Aaron and Joseph A. Pechman, *How Taxes Affect Economic Behavior*, Studies in Government Finance (Washington, D.C.: The Brookings Institution, 1981); and Laurence H. Meyer, ed., *The Supply Side Effects of Economic Policy*, Proceedings of the 1980 Economic Policy Conference, Center for Study of American Business and the Federal Reserve Bank of St. Louis.

5. Bartlett argues that the income effects cancel out in the aggregate. While this would be theoretically possible, the necessary assumptions for this to occur would be quite strong.

6. An important exception is Colin Wright, "Saving and the Rate of Interest," in A. C. Harberger and M. J. Bailey, eds., *The Taxation of Income from Capital* (Washington, D.C.: The Brookings Institution, 1969), pp. 275–95.

7. Recent summary articles on labor supply and savings elasticities include Boskin, op. cit.; Charles R. Hulten and June A. O'Neill, "Tax Policy," in John L. Palmer and Isabell V. Sawhill, eds., *The Reagan Experiment* (Washington, D.C.: The Urban Institute Press, 1982); and Mai Nguyen Woo, "Taxation, Savings, and Labor Supply: Theory and Evidence of Distortions," in Raboy, ed., op. cit.

8. Examples of the usual argument that tax cuts depress consumer demand, allowing for more investment and/or less inflation, can be found in Timothy Roth, "An Economic Analysis of the Reagan Plan for Economic Recovery," study for the Congressional Joint Economic Committee, 1981; and Timothy Roth and Mark Policinski, "Marginal Tax Rates, Savings, and the Federal Government Deficit," study for the Congressional Joint Economic Committee, 1981.

9. The elasticity of income to tax rates is not equivalent to the elasticity of labor hours to after-tax real wages. In fact, for a constant labor supply elasticity less than unity, the income tax rate elasticity should rise as the tax rate rises. This phenomenon gives the Laffer Curve its shape, in the classical labor demand-supply version. For an example in which the Laffer Curve hits a maximum at an 82 percent rate, see James Tobin, "Stabilization Policy Ten Years After," Brookings Papers on Economic Activity, no. 1, 1980, p. 40.

10. For a critique on the Roth, et al., thesis that tax cuts reduce consumer demand and the evidence they offer, see J. Harold McClure, "A Critique of Administration Views on Fiscal and Monetary Policy," mimeo, Claremont Graduate School Department of Economics, Claremont, Calif., 1982; and Tobin, op. cit.

11. Bartlett and Ture are quite explicit in their belief in classical economics and Say's Law. Demand policies will have no output effects, unless they create misperceptions of price movements. Both authors go even further by claiming that fiscal policy

has no demand effects either. Bartlett's rationale is grounded in Barro's belief that the budget must be balanced in the long run and that consumers realize this fact and act in an intergenerational life-cycle fashion. Changes in taxes will have zero effects on consumption in the extreme Barro model. The basis for Ture's belief is unclear. He may be leaping from the proposition that fiscal policy has no output effects to an assertion that it has no demand effects, when he argues that any supply effect from tax cuts will reduce inflation. Alternatively, Ture may be implicitly imposing vertical LM curves, but if that is the case, tax cuts completely crowd out investment.

12. Traditional macroeconomics has been a one-good, one-labor market approach. In a world of many markets, showing Keynesian unemployment in some markets does not preclude full employment in others. In such a case, aggregate output movements may be a mixture of both Keynesian demand and potential supply effects. A more disaggregated approach to macroeconomics is needed for such a case.

13. William Branson, for example, shows how tax rate cuts can raise tax revenues in a purely demand model. The formal condition is that the crowding-in minus crowding-out effects on investment from a one-unit rise in output exceed the marginal propensity to save. See William H. Branson, *Macroeconomic Theory and Policy* (New York: Harper and Row, 1972), pp. 288–93.

14. Rudiger Dornbusch and Stanley Fischer, *Macroeconomics* (Hightstown, N.J.: McGraw-Hill, 1978), pp. 304–308.

15. Joseph Minarik, "Capital Gains," in Aaron and Pechman, op. cit.

16. See Bartlett, for example.

5. Attiat F. Ott: "Controlling Government Spending"

1. Philip Cagan, "The Real Federal Deficit and Financial Markets," *AEI Economist* (1981).

2. W. N. Niskanen's views were aired during a seminar on economic policy sponsored by the American Enterprise Institute, 8 December 1981.

3. Allen Schick, "Controlling the Budget by Statute: An Imperfect but Workable Process," paper prepared for the Conference on Constraining Federal Taxing and Spending, sponsored by the Hoover Institution, 21–23 October 1981.

7. Wm. Craig Stubblebine: "The Economics of the New Federalism"

1. W. E. Oates, *Fiscal Federalism* (New York: Harcourt Brace Jovanovich, 1972), pp. 14–15.

2. Ibid., p. 34.

8. Thomas Gale Moore: "The Reagan Deregulation Program: An Assessment"

1. *Regulation,* January/February 1981, p. 35.

2. *Inside OMB,* 26 March 1982, pp. 1, 5–9.

3. *The Wall Street Journal,* 9 June 1981.

4. *Regulation,* November/December 1980, pp. 20–22.

5. *New York Times,* 9 June 1981, sec. IV, p. 1.

6. MC—127042, sub. 304; Hagen, Inc., Extension — General Commodities, Nationwide.

7. *Traffic World,* 22 February 1982, pp. 30—32.

8. Ibid.

9.   Michael J. Boskin: "Distributional Effects of the Reagan Program"

1. John L. Palmer and Isabel V. Sawhill, eds., *The Reagan Experiment* (Washington, D.C.: The Urban Institute Press, 1982).

2. See M. Boskin and E. Sheshinksi, "Optimal Redistributive Taxation When Individual Welfare Depends upon Relative Income," *Quarterly Journal of Economics* (1978).

3. A. Harberger, "On the Use of Distributional Weights in Social Cost-Benefit Analysis," *Journal of Political Economy* (April 1978): S87—S120.

CONTRIBUTORS

HENRY J. AARON is a senior fellow at the Brookings Institution and professor of economics at the University of Maryland. For nearly two years he was assistant secretary for planning and evaluation in the Department of Health, Education, and Welfare during the Carter administration. His most recent books are *The Value-Added Tax: Lessons from Europe* (1981) and *Economic Effects of Social Security* (1982).

DAVID BERSON is a visiting scholar at the Federal Reserve Bank of Kansas City for 1983, on leave from the faculty of the economics department of Claremont McKenna College. He was formerly a staff economist for the Council of Economic Advisers and for the Treasury Department's Office of Tax Analysis.

MICHAEL J. BOSKIN, professor of economics at Stanford University and research associate for the National Bureau of Economic Research, is an authority on taxation and public finance. He was a member of the Reagan campaign task forces on tax policy and social security and has served as consultant to the Department of Health and Human Services, the Department of Defense, and the U.S. Treasury. He has written extensively on taxation, social security, econometrics, and labor economics, and is editor of two Institute publications—*The Crisis in Social Security* and *Federal Tax Reform,* both published in 1978.

WILLIAM H. BRANSON is professor of economics at the Woodrow Wilson School of Princeton University, and has been director of research in international economics and research associate for the National Bureau of Economic Research. A consultant to various agencies of the United States and foreign governments, he is also coeditor of the *Journal of International Economics,* associate editor of several other journals, and the author of a number of works dealing with international economics.

217

JACOB DREYER has been the assistant deputy for monetary policy analysis in the U.S. Treasury Department since March 1982. Formerly acting deputy assistant secretary for international economic analysis and director of the Office of Monetary Research and Quantitative Studies, he has taught economics at New York University and is the author of a number of publications.

ROSS D. ECKERT is professor of economics at Claremont McKenna College and adjunct scholar at the American Enterprise Institute. He has also been a consultant to government agencies and has written several books and numerous articles on economic regulation, natural resources, and transportation, including *The Enclosure of Ocean Resources: Economics and the Law of the Sea* (1979).

SUSAN FEIGENBAUM is an applied econometrician with a particular interest in the relative efficiency of alternative economic institutions. An assistant professor of economics at Claremont McKenna College and the Claremont Graduate Center, she has recently published papers on the nonprofit voluntary sector and the comparative behavior of governmental and private water delivery systems.

ARTHUR B. LAFFER is the Charles B. Thornton Professor of Business Economics at the University of Southern California. He is also a member of the President's Policy Advisory Board and of the *Los Angeles Times* Board of Economists.

J. HAROLD McCLURE has been assistant professor of economics at Claremont Graduate School since 1981. He has written a number of papers for the Claremont Working Paper series, including "Reagan's Fiscal and Monetary Policies: A Critique of the Views of the Joint Economic Committee and Other Reaganomics Proponents" and, with Thomas D. Willett, "A Demand and Supply-Side Rejoinder to the Case for Radical Supply-Side Economics."

THOMAS G. MOORE, senior fellow and director of domestic studies at the Hoover Institution, is also a consultant to the U.S. Department of Transportation and the Synthetic Fuels Corporation. Recently he was a member of President Reagan's pre-election task forces on energy policy and regulatory policy as well as the transition team on the Interstate Commerce Commission. He was formerly a senior staff economist on the Council of Economic Advisers for presidents Johnson and Nixon, and professor of economics at Michigan State University.

PEGGY B. MUSGRAVE, professor of economics at the University of California at Santa Cruz, has written extensively in the field of public finance, especially in the area of taxation of foreign investment income. She is the coauthor, with Richard A. Musgrave, of *Public Finance in Theory and Practice* (1973).

RICHARD A. MUSGRAVE is H. H. Burbank Professor of Political Economy Emeritus at Harvard University and adjunct professor of economics at the University of California at Santa Cruz. A Distinguished Fellow of the American Economic Association, he is the author of *The Theory of Public Finance* (1959) and, jointly with Peggy B. Musgrave, of *Public Finance in Theory and Practice* (1973).

WILLIAM A. NISKANEN has been a member of the Council of Economic Advisers since April 1981, with particular responsibility for analyses of policy areas such as regulations, subsidies, labor, and trade that affect selected sectors of the economy. He has taught at the University of California at Berkeley and Los Angeles; has worked for the Office of Management and Budget, the Defense Department, and the Ford Motor Company; and has been active in the movement to enact a Constitutional amendment limiting taxes. His works include *Bureaucracy and Representative Government* and a number of articles on a range of policy issues.

WALLACE E. OATES became a professor of economics at the University of Maryland in 1979, after fourteen years of teaching at Princeton. He is the author of *Fiscal Federalism* (1972) and other books and articles on public finance and on the economics of environmental policy.

ATTIAT F. OTT is professor of economics and director of policy studies of the Institute for Economic Studies, Clark University. She is also a member of the Advisory Board of Tax Advocates and Analysts in Washington, D.C., and an adjunct scholar and member of the Technical Advisory Board (Tax Studies) at the American Enterprise Institute. Formerly a Brookings research associate, a scholar in residence at the Organization for Economic Cooperation and Development (OECD) in Paris, and a visiting scholar at the Hoover Institution, she has held academic appointments at the University of Maryland, Southern Methodist University, and Cairo University. Her many publications include *The Federal Budget Policy* (1977); *The Income Tax Burden on Households* (1981); "The Growth of Government in the West," in *Taxing and Spending Policy,* Samuels and Wade, eds. (1980); and "The Measurement of

Government Saving" and "Capital Formation by Government" in *The Government and Capital Formation,* Von Furstenberg, ed. (1980).

RICHARD W. RAHN joined the U.S. Chamber of Commerce in 1980 as vice-president and chief economist, and is also director and vice-president of the National Chamber Foundation. He has been executive director of the American Council for Capital Formation and chief executive officer of the council's Center for Policy Research; managing director of the Ripon Society; and president of the National Capital chapter of the National Association of Business Economists. From 1966–1973 he was associate professor and head of the Graduate Department of Management at the Polytechnic Institute of New York, during which time he also had the opportunity to serve as administrator of the AID-sponsored Rural Industrial Technical Assistance Program in Brazil.

ALICE RIVLIN, director of the Congressional Budget Office, has previously been associated with a variety of government agencies and with the Brookings Institution. She is the author of five books and studies, including *Systematic Thinking for Social Action* (1971) and, jointly with Charles L. Schultze, et al., of *Setting National Priorities* (1971, 1972, and 1973).

BERYL W. SPRINKEL is the Reagan administration's undersecretary of the Treasury for monetary affairs. Before joining the administration, he was executive vice-president and economist of Harris Bank in Chicago, where he was also director of the bank's economic and financial forecasting service. He is the author of *Money and Stock Prices* (1964) and *Money and Markets— A Monetarist View* (1971), and is coauthor with Bob Genetski of *Winning with Money* (1977).

Wm. CRAIG STUBBLEBINE, since 1979 the Von Tobel Professor of Political Economy and director of the Center for the Study of Law Structures at Claremont McKenna College and Claremont Graduate School, is an expert in the field of tax limitation. He was a founding director of the National Tax Limitation Committee and chairs the national committee that drafted the proposed federal spending limitation amendment now before Congress, in addition to serving as consultant to various state limitation drafting committees. In 1967–68 he was the Fulbright Lecturer in Welfare Economics at the University of Turin, Italy, and has taught at a number of universities. He has written and lectured extensively in the areas of property rights, public finance, welfare economics, and public choice, and most recently contributed to the Institute's *American Federalism: A New Partnership for the Republic* (1982).

ROBERT TOLLISON is director of the Bureau of Economics at the Federal Trade Commission and on leave from Clemson University, where he is Abney Professor of Economics. Formerly executive director of the Center for the Study of Public Choice at Virginia Polytechnic Institute, he has written widely in the areas of public choice and industrial organization. His two most recent books are *Politicians, Legislation, and the Economy* (with Robert McCormick) and *Mercantilism as a Rent-Seeking Society* (with Robert Ekelund), both published in 1982.

THOMAS D. WILLETT, Horton Professor of Economics at the Claremont Graduate School and Claremont McKenna College, is a noted specialist in international economic affairs. Before joining the Claremont faculties in 1977, he served in the U.S. Treasury as deputy assistant secretary for international research and planning. His teaching credentials include positions at the University of Virginia, Harvard University, the Kennedy School of Government (Harvard University), the Fletcher School of Law and Diplomacy, and Cornell University. A prolific writer, he has served on the editorial boards of a number of scholarly journals, most recently the *International Studies Quarterly* and *International Organization.*

INDEX